THE **I'M IN THE MOOD FOR** COOKBOOK

THE **I'M IN THE MOOD FOR** COOKBOOK

THE COOKBOOK
THAT ANSWERS
THE QUESTION,
"WHAT DO
YOU FEEL LIKE
EATING?"

Library of Congress Cataloging in Publication Data
Main entry under title:

The I'm in the mood for cookbook.

   Copyright held by Wear-Ever Aluminum, Inc.
   Includes index.
   1. Cookery. 2. Kitchen utensils. I. Wear-Ever Aluminum, Inc.
TX652.I45   641.5   81.20231
ISBN 0-911974-29-6 (pbk.)   AACR2

THE RECIPES IN THIS COOKBOOK WERE SPECIALLY CREATED IN THE WEAR-EVER KITCHENS AND THE CREATIVE KITCHENS OF CAROL MOBERG COMMUNICATIONS.
PHOTOGRAPHY OF SELECTED RECIPES BY GUS FRANCISCO/ALLEN BAILLIE PHOTOGRAPHY, INC.

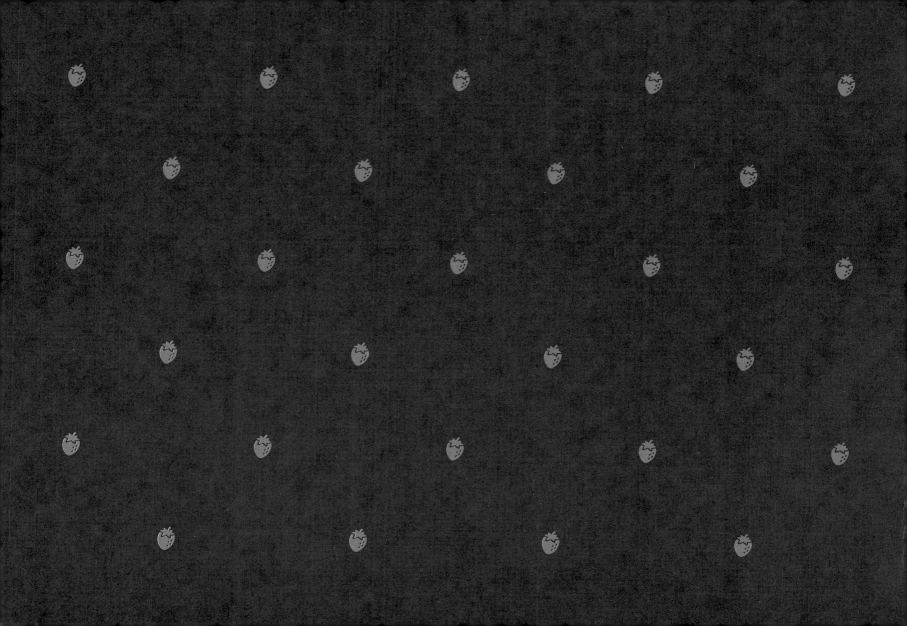

CONTENTS

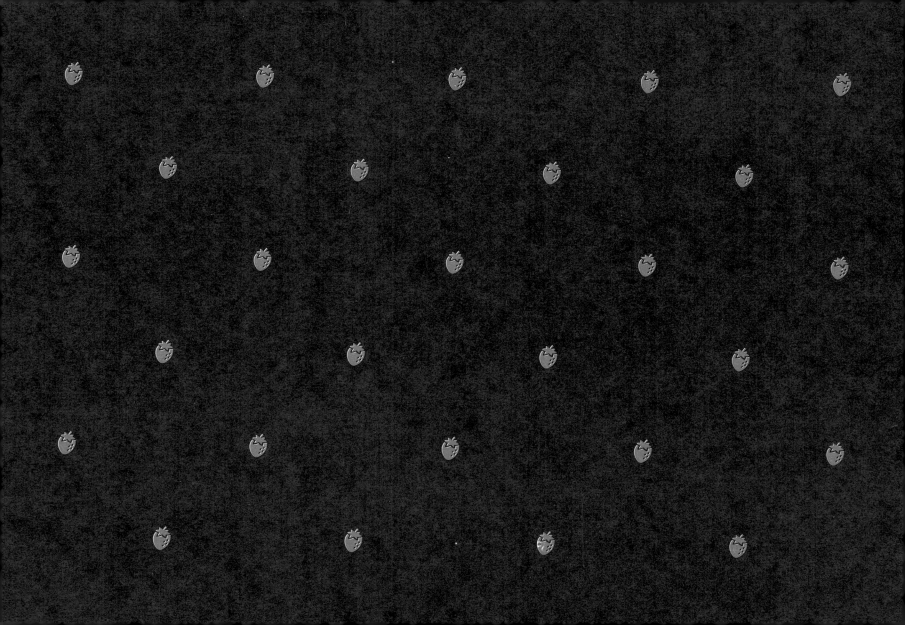

INTRODUCTION

Once upon a time, meals were created from local game and home-grown produce, and recipes were handed down within the traditions of one's own culture.

Today, when you walk down the aisle of a supermarket you see the tremendous variety of choices available to American cooks. The average chain supermarket now stocks more than 10,000 items, including packaged goods and produce from all over the world, allowing you to bring a multitude of ethnic flavors to the table.

Blessed with these choices, today's cooks can satisfy much more than the basic need to eat. More people than ever before are discovering that cooking can be a creative outlet, a way to make a statement about themselves, and an expression of their feelings.

Food is a reflection of the individual cook's style and imagination. Almost inevitably when you want to know what others want to eat, you ask, "What do you feel like?" or "What are you in the mood for?"

This book was inspired by these questions and organized accordingly. A casual look at the tables of contents of other cookbooks would show chapters devoted to "Appetizers" or "Main Dishes" or "Desserts." This one is different. Instead of categorizing recipes according to the course, we have classified them by the basic feelings that we think they will complement. Here are a few points to consider when you use this cookbook.

We selected and developed recipes to fit a feeling, mood or situation suggested by each chapter. Most chapters also contain several ideas for each course, so it's often possible to plan a complete meal from one chapter.

If you are planning to give a party, we hope you will find some culinary inspiration in "Celebration." If you're dining alone tomorrow evening and are tempted to satisfy your hunger with take-out corned beef from the deli, it's possible that "The Pleasure of Your Own Company" will keep you happily at home with an easy-to-prepare, satisfying meal.

If you have a yen for "back to basics" cooking, turn to "The Itch to Make It from Scratch." This chapter contains fifteen recipes that will satisfy this urge. Most of the "scratch" recipes are for items that are packaged and available commercially. Also, you will note that throughout this cookbook such convenience items are marked with a chef's toque (♟). The toque indicates that you will find a recipe for that ingredient in the "scratch" chapter.

Some of the recipes in "A Family Affair" contain steps that you can teach your children to master even before they are ready to be involved in actual cooking. Turn to page 18 for these ideas on how to get kids started in the kitchen.

Have you ever wondered why the dishes in elegant continental restaurants look so terrific? The technique of arranging an attractive plate is called "garnishing." Read page 105 to learn how to make your meals as appealing as those of a master chef.

Throughout the book, and in the sections beginning on pages 107 and 111, cooking tips and menu suggestions offer some basic guidelines on enhancing your cooking skills, as well as some fascinating facts and helpful hints on ingredients and preparation. The menu section also contains suggestions for planning complete meals, with some recommendations on wine.

And finally, a whole chapter is devoted to Wear-Ever® products. All of the recipes in *The I'm in the Mood for Cookbook* have been developed for and tested with Wear-Ever Cookware and Bakeware with SilverStone* and Wear-Ever specialty electric appliances. You will achieve the best results with these recipes by using the exact piece of equipment that is called for.

We hope you enjoy this somewhat unusual approach to cooking and that you will refer to this cookbook whenever you are "in the mood for" something imaginative and fun to cook! ■

® Trademark of Wear-Ever Aluminum, Inc.
*DuPont's registered trademark for its premium non-stick surface.

A FAMILY AFFAIR

"Hey, Mom, can I help you cook?"

"Sure, do you know how to break an egg?"

"No, but I'm great at licking the bowl!"

So many warm family memories are centered around kitchen activity that the kitchen holds a special place in our hearts. Food and the kitchen are still central to most of our lives.

The warm glow of family togetherness is no longer consigned to distant memories. Kitchens today are beginning to reflect the growing interest and need of busy, working families to be close during those few hours they are home together.

The kitchen is no longer the woman's domain. Just as early American families shared the task of food preparation, husbands and children are assuming a larger part of the cook's role. Cooking has become a family affair and the kitchen has become the new family room.

The recipes in this chapter are an assortment of variations on family favorites—foods that will help start your own family traditions, like pizza for Sunday nights, moussaka for when relatives visit or lasagna for a special treat.

A few of the recipes will help you introduce your children to the joys of cooking, not only for themselves, but for others. Little hands can tackle meatballs, cookies or granola with confidence and then learn the satisfaction of sharing their treasures with the rest of the family.

Even in an age of working parents and independent children, the kitchen is still one room that inspires togetherness and sharing. And that's what the best memories are made of. ■

11

12

ALPHABET SOUP

Kids can learn the letters, and learn to like vegetables, too!

½	cup butter or margarine
¼	cup vegetable oil
3	medium onions, finely chopped
4	medium carrots, finely chopped
2	stalks celery, finely chopped
2	cloves garlic, minced
1	can (8-oz) peeled tomatoes
2	large potatoes, peeled, diced
4	medium zucchini, diced
1½	teaspoons salt
¾	teaspoon basil
½	teaspoon oregano
½	teaspoon rosemary
¼	teaspoon pepper
3	quarts water
2	beef bouillon cubes
1	pound frozen lima beans
½	cup alphabet shape pasta
½	cup grated Parmesan cheese

1. Heat butter, oil in *8½-quart Sauce Pot* over medium heat; add onions, carrots, celery, garlic; sauté vegetables until tender.

2. Add tomatoes, potatoes, zucchini, salt, basil, oregano, rosemary, pepper; bring to boil; cover; reduce heat to low; simmer 20 minutes, stirring occasionally.

3. Add water, bouillon cubes; bring to boil over medium-high heat; cover; reduce heat to low; simmer 2 hours; add lima beans, pasta; continue to cook 30 minutes longer; sprinkle with Parmesan.

Makes 4 quarts

FRENCH ONION SOUP

The classic hearty recipe; kids love the gooey cheese on top!

1	cup butter or margarine
12	large onions (4-lb), sliced
2	tablespoons sugar
3	quarts (96-oz) canned chicken broth
¼	cup Cognac or brandy (optional)
12	slices French bread, toasted
1½	cups shredded Swiss cheese

1. Melt butter in *5-quart Dutch Oven* over medium heat; sauté onions for 15 minutes; add sugar; continue cooking 20-25 minutes or until golden brown.

2. Add broth; bring to boil; cover; simmer 45 minutes; add Cognac.

3. Ladle soup into individual heat-proof bowls; add bread slice to each bowl; top with cheese; place under broiler 3 minutes or until cheese melts, browns.

Makes 4 quarts

PIZZA BIANCA

Deep-dish, gooey pie for the cheese-lovers in your house.

2	loaves (1-lb each) frozen bread dough, thawed
2	containers (15-oz each) ricotta cheese
8	ounces shredded mozzarella cheese
1	cup grated Parmesan cheese
8	ounces pepperoni, thinly sliced

1. Thaw dough and knead following package directions; roll dough into a thick rectangle about 19 x 14 inches; fit dough into *Au Gratin Pan,* pressing firmly onto bottom, sides; pinch excess at top to stand a little above top edge of pan, similar to a pie crust.

2. Combine ricotta, mozzarella, Parmesan with ½ the pepperoni; spread over dough in pan.

3. Bake 10 minutes at 400°F.; arrange remaining pepperoni over top; continue baking 10-15 minutes or until nicely browned; serve in pan or slide out onto serving platter; cut in wedges. (Not a finger food.)

Makes 6-8 servings

13

MOUSSAKA
Adaptation of the traditional Greek lamb and eggplant casserole.

- **3** medium eggplants (about 3-lb)
- **¼** cup olive oil
- **3** cups finely chopped onions
- **3** pounds ground lamb or beef
- **2** cups (16-oz) canned tomato sauce
- **⅔** cup red wine
- **1½** teaspoons cinnamon
- **1½** teaspoons nutmeg
- **2** tablespoons olive oil
- **1** cup grated Parmesan cheese
- **6** cups medium white sauce
- **2** eggs, slightly beaten
- **1** cup fresh bread crumbs
- **3** cups grated Parmesan cheese

1. Cut eggplant crosswise into ⅛-inch slices; arrange slices in *15½ x 11 x 2-inch Bake & Roast Pan* by resting them upright around sides of pan, then continue making rows with remaining slices—pan will be full; sprinkle with 1 cup water; cover with aluminum foil; bake 30 minutes at 400°F. or until tender; lay slices on paper towels to drain.

2. Heat oil in *12-inch Chef Style Fry Pan* over medium heat; sauté onions until golden brown; add meat; sauté until meat is lightly browned; drain off excess fat; add tomato sauce, wine, cinnamon, nutmeg; simmer 12-15 minutes or until most of liquid is absorbed.

3. Brush bottom of bake pan with oil; arrange ½ the eggplant slices across bottom—slices will overlap; spread with meat mixture; sprinkle with Parmesan; cover with remaining eggplant slices.

4. In large bowl, combine white sauce, eggs, crumbs, Parmesan; spread over eggplant; bake 50 minutes at 350°F. or until top is browned, mixture barely set in center; remove from oven; cover with aluminum foil; allow to stand 30 minutes before serving.

Makes 12 servings

BOSTON-STYLE FISH CAKES
Much lighter and fluffier than frozen fish cakes.

- **1** pound cod fillets, boned
- **1** bay leaf
- **2** cups finely chopped onions
- **3½** cups mashed potatoes
- **½** cup chopped fresh parsley
- **2** teaspoons Worcestershire sauce
- **¼** teaspoon salt
- **¼** teaspoon pepper
  Pinch cloves
- **2** eggs
- **2** tablespoons vegetable oil
- **2** cups dry bread crumbs
- **½** cup chopped fresh parsley
- **1** cup flour
- **¼** cup vegetable oil

1. Place fish fillets in *3-quart Sauce Pan;* cover with salted water; add bay leaf, onions; simmer 20 minutes or until tender; drain; discard bay leaf.

2. In large bowl, combine fish, mashed potatoes, parsley, Worcestershire, salt, pepper, cloves; beat with electric mixer until thoroughly blended; shape mixture into fourteen 3 x ½-inch thick cakes.

3. Beat eggs with oil; combine crumbs, parsley; coat fish cakes with flour; dip into egg mixture; coat with crumbs.

4. Heat oil in *11-inch Chicken Fryer* over medium heat; place 7 cakes in pan; fry 8 minutes per side or until golden brown; repeat with remaining cakes; serve with your favorite sauce, as desired.

Makes 14

VEGETARIAN LASAGNA
Walnuts and cheese provide the protein in this delicious meatless recipe.

½	pound lasagna noodles
½	cup olive oil
2	cups (½-lb) chopped walnuts
2	cups chopped onions
1	cup chopped green pepper
3	cloves garlic, minced
3½	cups (28-oz) canned tomato sauce
1	teaspoon basil
½	teaspoon oregano
1	container (15-oz) ricotta cheese
8	ounces sliced mozzarella cheese
½	cup grated Parmesan cheese

1. Cook lasagna noodles in *5-quart Dutch Oven* following package directions; rinse in cold water; drain.

2. Heat oil in *12-inch Chef Style Fry Pan* over medium heat; add walnuts; cook 5 minutes or until lightly browned; remove with slotted spoon; reserve.

3. Add onions, green pepper, garlic to pan; sauté until onions are translucent; add tomato sauce, basil, oregano; simmer 5 minutes.

4. *To assemble:* Spread ⅓ sauce in bottom of *11½ x 9 x 2-inch Bake & Roast Pan;* layer ingredients as follows: ½ noodles, all ricotta, ½ walnuts, ⅓ sauce, all mozzarella, remaining noodles, walnuts, sauce; sprinkle Parmesan over top.

5. Cover pan with aluminum foil; bake 30 minutes at 350°F.; remove foil; bake additional 10-15 minutes; let stand 10 minutes before cutting.

Makes 6-8 servings

Variations:
- May add 2 jars drained, marinated artichoke hearts.
- May substitute green lasagna noodles, if available.
- May add 2 cups cooked, sliced mushrooms, chopped spinach or broccoli.
- May add 1 pound cooked, crumbled sweet Italian sausage or ground beef to sauce.

MEXICAN MEATBALLS
Spicy pork meatballs with a south-of-the-border sauce.

3	pounds ground pork
3	cups fresh bread crumbs
1	cup finely chopped onions
2	eggs
2	teaspoons salt
1	teaspoon cumin
1	teaspoon oregano
1	teaspoon pepper
3	medium green peppers
2	cups (16-oz) canned tomato sauce
1	tablespoon sugar
1	tablespoon chopped green chili peppers
1	teaspoon cumin

1. Combine pork, crumbs, onions, eggs, salt, cumin, oregano, pepper; blend thoroughly; form mixture into sixty-four 1¼-inch diameter balls (about 1½ tablespoons each); refrigerate 1 hour.

2. Cut green peppers into sixty-four 1-inch pieces; allowing a 1-inch space from skewer handle, thread 4 green pepper pieces and 4 meatballs alternately on each skewer; attach skewer guards.

3. Combine tomato sauce, sugar, chili peppers, cumin; blend thoroughly; brush on meatballs.

4. Insert skewers into *Kabob-It* base; place glass cover over food; kabob 28-30 minutes or until nicely browned; repeat with remaining ingredients; heat remaining sauce; serve with meatballs.

Makes 16 servings

15

PASTA PRIMAVERA
Use garden-fresh vegetables for this traditional spring recipe.

- 12 **asparagus spears (3" pieces)**
- 2 **cups sliced green beans (1" pieces)**
- 2 **cups pea pods**
- ½ **cup vegetable oil**
- 1 **cup chopped green onions**
- 3 **large cloves garlic, minced**
- 2 **cups tomatoes, peeled, seeded, diced (1-lb)**
- 2 **cups sliced mushrooms (4-oz)**
- 1 **cup medium white sauce** 🍳
- 1 **cup half & half**
- 1 **teaspoon oregano**
- 1 **teaspoon basil**
- 1½ **cups grated Parmesan cheese**
- 1 **pound spaghetti**
- 1 **cup chopped parsley**
- ⅔ **cup pine nuts (optional)**

1. Pour 1-inch water in *12-inch Chef Style Fry Pan;* bring to boil; steam vegetables in batches until tender-crisp, as follows — asparagus 12 minutes; green beans 10 minutes; pea pods 3 minutes; reserve; pour off water.

2. In same pan, heat oil over medium heat; add green onions, garlic; sauté 3-4 minutes; add tomatoes, mushrooms; cook 2 additional minutes; add white sauce, half & half, oregano, basil; simmer 15 minutes; stir in Parmesan until melted.

3. Cook spaghetti in *8½-quart Sauce Pot* following package directions; drain; return to pot; add steamed vegetables, sauce, parsley; toss gently to blend; garnish with pine nuts; serve immediately.

Makes 8 servings

Variation:
May use any combination fresh or frozen vegetables available.

BLUEBERRY PANCAKES
A favorite family breakfast treat.

- 1 **cup pancake mix** 🍳
- ½ **cup blueberries**
- 1 **teaspoon brown sugar**
- ½ **teaspoon almond extract**

1. Prepare pancake mix following package directions; stir in blueberries, brown sugar, almond extract. (When using frozen or canned blueberries, drain thoroughly and pat dry.)

2. Place *Double Griddle* over two units of range; preheat over medium heat about 2 minutes or until drops of water dance on dry griddle surface.

3. Pour batter by ¼ cupful onto ungreased griddle (6 at a time); turn cakes after 2 minutes or when bubbles break on top; continue cooking about 1 minute or until cakes are golden brown — adjust heat as needed.

Makes 12

Variations:
One of the following may be substituted for blueberries: any small berry, chopped nuts, chocolate chips.

TIP:

Pancakes and crepes may be prepared in advance and kept warm by layering between folded kitchen towels and placing in a 200°F. oven until ready to eat.

16

SOUTHERN-STYLE CORNBREAD

Topped with maple syrup, it's an all-American favorite.

2½	cups yellow cornmeal
½	cup flour
1½	teaspoons baking soda
¾	teaspoon salt
3	eggs, beaten
1	cup buttermilk
1½	cups milk
3	tablespoons butter or margarine
½	cup milk

1. Thoroughly blend cornmeal, flour, baking soda, salt; combine eggs, buttermilk, milk; stir egg mixture into dry ingredients until blended.

2. Melt butter over medium heat in *11½ x 9 x 2-inch Bake & Roast Pan;* pour batter into pan; spread evenly; carefully pour milk over top.

3. Bake 1 hour at 350°F. or until cornbread is set; cut into serving pieces; serve with butter, maple syrup, as desired.

Makes 8-12 servings

COUNTRY GRANOLA

Tastier than store-bought; everyone will want to eat breakfast!

5½	cups quick-cooking oats
2	cups flaked coconut
2	cups chopped nuts
½	cup butter or margarine
½	cup light brown sugar
½	cup honey
1	tablespoon vanilla
⅔	cup vacuum packed wheat germ
1½	cups raisins

1. Combine oats, coconut, nuts in *15½ x 11 x 2-inch Bake & Roast Pan;* bake 20 minutes at 300°F., tossing occasionally.

2. Melt butter in *2-quart Sauce Pan;* add brown sugar, honey; remove from heat; add vanilla.

3. Add wheat germ to oats; drizzle with butter mixture; toss together; bake 5 minutes at 350°F.

4. Add raisins; toss together; press mixture into pan; bake additional 5-7 minutes; cool; store in air-tight container.

Makes 12 cups

Variations:
Add ½ cup of any one of the following, as desired: dried pineapple, chopped apricots, chopped apples, sunflower seeds.

BANANA WALNUT BREAD

A moist treat that's even better the next day!

1½	cups butter or margarine
1⅓	cups sugar
4	eggs
2	cups mashed bananas (about 4)
3½	cups all purpose flour
4	teaspoons baking powder
½	teaspoon baking soda
½	teaspoon nutmeg
1	cup coarsely chopped walnuts

1. With electric mixer, beat butter, sugar together; add eggs; beat well; blend in bananas.

2. Thoroughly blend flour, baking powder, baking soda, nutmeg; gradually stir dry ingredients into banana mixture; fold in nuts.

3. Pour batter into two lightly greased *8½ x 4 x 3-inch Loaf Pans;* bake 1¼ hours at 350°F. or until done, golden brown.

Makes 2 loaves

17

18

LEMON WAFER COOKIES

Delicate, melt in your mouth treats; watch them disappear!

1	cup butter or margarine
1	cup sugar
1	egg, slightly beaten
2	tablespoons grated lemon peel
1	tablespoon fresh lemon juice
1¾	cups all purpose flour
1	teaspoon baking soda
1	teaspoon cream of tartar
½	teaspoon salt
	Sugar

1. With electric mixer, beat butter, sugar together; add egg, lemon peel, lemon juice; blend well.

2. Thoroughly blend flour, baking soda, cream of tartar, salt; gradually stir into lemon mixture; wrap dough in plastic film; refrigerate 5 hours or until stiff.

3. Form dough into sixty ¾-inch balls (1 teaspoon each); place on ungreased *15½ x 12-inch Cookie Sheets,* allowing 12 balls per sheet; cover bottom of glass with damp towel; dip glass into sugar; press down on cookies to flatten to make 2-inch circles.

4. Bake 8-12 minutes at 325°F. or until golden brown around edges; cool slightly before removing from cookie sheets; finish cooling on wire racks.

Makes 5 dozen

CHOCOLATE-ORANGE TORTE

An easy "make-ahead" dessert using packaged cookies.

3½	squares semi-sweet chocolate
3	eggs, separated
1	teaspoon vanilla
1	teaspoon grated orange peel
26	chocolate wafer cookies
2	tablespoons orange juice
½	square semi-sweet chocolate
½	cup non-dairy whipped topping

1. Melt chocolate in *1-quart Sauce Pan* over medium-low heat; remove from heat; stir in egg yolks, vanilla, orange peel; beat egg whites until stiff but not dry; fold chocolate mixture into whites.

2. Arrange ½ the cookies in bottom of *8-inch Round Cake Pan;* sprinkle with 1 tablespoon orange juice; spoon on ½ chocolate mixture; repeat above layers with remaining cookies, orange juice, chocolate mixture; cover; place in refrigerator 5 hours or overnight.

3. To serve: Loosen around edge with hot knife; dip bottom of pan in hot water, then turn torte out; place upright on serving dish.

4. Coarsely grate chocolate; pat on sides of torte; place whipped topping in barrel of *Super Shooter;* garnish top of torte using decorator tip.

Makes 8 servings

TEACHING KIDS TO COOK

Youngsters in a sand pile reveal their fascination with cooking by making mud pies. As children grow, they can be introduced to the world of real cooking, expanding their skills according to their ability and desire to learn.

There are a few guidelines and activities which will ensure your children's safety as you introduce them to the culinary arts.

USING EQUIPMENT

Although children will want to practice the skills that you teach them, under no circumstances should they be allowed to operate appliances or use sharp implements without adult supervision. In fact, it is usually much better to wait until youngsters reach adolescence before teaching them this type of kitchen work. Instead of these complex tasks, begin by teaching the most basic operations in food preparation. Cover your kitchen table with a washable cloth or mat, give your children aprons, and watch them enjoy doing the following simple cooking tasks.

Continued

• Mixing

Wooden spoons, plastic bowls with handles, and clean, dry hands are all that are needed to show your children how to stir ingredients together. To help prepare the recipe for Mexican Meatballs in this chapter, your children can mix the ground meat and seasoning with their hands—a truly simple exercise. They'll also have fun shaping the meatballs!

Don't assign your children a tricky mixture, like a baking batter, as a learning experience. Kids may be overzealous at first when mixing and stirring, and will be disappointed if the recipe doesn't succeed.

• Measuring

Fractions are a headache for many children, but working with kitchen measuring utensils is a practical learning experience that will help them in math class.

Demonstrate the various sizes of liquid and dry measuring cups, scoops and spoons. Show your children each of the different measures called for in a recipe, and then let them help you measure the ingredients.

• Cutting

Since mincing, dicing and chopping require the use of a sharp knife, or food processor, they are not appropriate kitchen tasks for children. However, many soft foods and vegetables (e.g. bananas, summer fruits) can be sliced with a plastic knife so children can begin learning these skills without endangering themselves. Children will also have fun pulling apart lettuce leaves for salads, since this is a job that requires no utensils.

SOME KITCHEN TASKS KIDS REALLY ENJOY

Rolling cookie dough or making bread crumbs by repeated rolling over toasted dry bread slices (placed between sheets of waxed paper) are tasks that children love. Select a rolling pin for them that is light and easy to use; your own may be too large and heavy.

Frosting cakes, cupcakes or cookies is also fun for children (if you can live with a less-than-beautiful result). They can use a blunt spreading spatula (plastic or metal) and feel quite proud of their accomplishment.

ABOUT CLEAN-UP

After the basic safety rules, the next most important kitchen rule to teach your children is always to clean up after cooking. Not only does this give them responsibility, but it will also spare you the headaches that a messy kitchen can provoke. Teach children to use a damp sponge to wipe up spills as soon as they occur.

Teaching youngsters about cooking rewards parents, too. An early positive experience with cooking means your children are likely to continue to be helpful in the kitchen when they are old enough to take responsibility for meal preparation and let mom and dad relax. More important, getting kids involved in the kitchen early in life may be their introduction to a skill that often becomes an enjoyable hobby in adulthood.

CELEBRATION

"Can you two come for dinner tomorrow? Bill's promotion came through and we're inviting some friends to celebrate."

"Sure! But how can you put a party together that quickly?"

"I'll share my secrets tomorrow!"

We all get the urge to celebrate at least several times a year. Birthdays, holidays, anniversaries and milestones such as raises and promotions are all occasions that can inspire us to bring friends together.

Too often, though, parties are perceived as time-consuming and expensive endeavors; many would-be partygivers have soured on the idea because their last party meal was so complex that they spent the whole evening minding the stove.

None of these drawbacks need stop you from giving your next party if you remember a few basic points about enjoying your own celebration.

First, always plan a party menu with recipes that you have tried before. New recipes—especially complex ones—can lead to last-minute panic if a sauce curdles, the yeast bread fails to rise or you forget a key step or ingredient.

Next, try to draw up a menu with a majority of recipes that can be prepared ahead of time and need only a reheating or decorative garnish. This will free you from the kitchen to enjoy the festivities.

And finally, if you are worried about the high cost of entertaining, don't break the bank by ordering a rack of lamb for ten. Instead, use less expensive cuts of meat that can be combined with other ingredients to make attractive, but penny-wise, dishes.

Most of the recipes in this chapter are designed to serve at least eight people. Many can be prepared ahead of time and frozen till the day of the party; others are relatively "fuss-free" and won't steal your time after guests arrive.

So, when you feel the urge to share your "special occasion" with friends, don't hesitate—celebrate! ■

21

COLD WATERCRESS SOUP

A delicious creamy soup, with the peppery taste of watercress.

1 **pound potatoes, peeled, quartered**
2 **cups chopped onions**
3 **medium zucchini, thickly sliced**
6 **cups (48-oz) canned chicken broth**
2 **bunches watercress, stems removed (2 cups)**
2 **tablespoons lemon juice**
1 **cup heavy cream**
  Salt, pepper
¼ **cup chopped chives**

1. Combine potatoes, onions, zucchini, chicken broth in *5-quart Dutch Oven;* cover; bring to boil over medium heat; reduce heat to low; simmer 40 minutes or until potatoes are soft; add watercress, lemon juice; simmer 3-5 minutes longer or until watercress is limp.

2. Allow mixture to cool, then ladle into blender container, in several batches; blend on low speed until smooth; add cream; season with salt, pepper to taste; refrigerate; serve well-chilled; garnish with chives.

Makes 3 quarts

CHICKEN LIVER MOUSSE

Rich buttery spread, flavored with Cognac and served on crackers.

1 **cup (8-oz) canned chicken broth**
1 **sprig fresh parsley**
¼ **cup chopped onions**
1 **tablespoon soy sauce**
1 **pound chicken livers**
½ **cup butter, softened**
1 **tablespoon Cognac or brandy**
1 **teaspoon salt**
½ **teaspoon dry mustard**
¼ **teaspoon ginger**
  Salt

1. Combine broth, parsley, onions, soy sauce in *2-quart Sauce Pan;* bring to boil over medium heat; add chicken livers; reduce heat to low; cover; simmer 15 minutes or until just tender; remove from heat; let cool.

2. Remove chicken livers with slotted spoon; place in blender container with enough liquid from pan to blend until very smooth (¼-½ cup); blend in butter, Cognac, salt, dry mustard, ginger; season with salt to taste; place mixture in serving dish; cover; refrigerate overnight; serve on a variety of crackers or bread.

Makes 2½ cups

MARINATED MUSHROOMS

These will keep several days in the refrigerator.

2 **pounds fresh button mushrooms**
1 **cup water**
1 **cup white wine**
¼ **cup lemon juice**
4 **teaspoons salt**
12 **peppercorns**
2 **bay leaves**
½ **teaspoon thyme**
½ **teaspoon coriander**
  Boston lettuce leaves

1. Combine all ingredients except lettuce in *5-quart Dutch Oven;* bring to boil over medium heat; reduce heat to low; simmer 5-7 minutes or until just tender; cool slightly; pour into shallow bowl; cover; refrigerate overnight.

2. Serve chilled mushrooms on lettuce as an appetizer.

Makes 10-12 servings

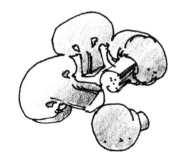

COQ AU VIN
*The traditional French "chicken stew" —
perfect for winter nights.*

1	pound bacon (1″ pieces)
3	pounds chicken legs
3	pounds chicken breasts, halved
	Flour
½	gallon red wine
24	small white onions
5	cloves garlic, minced
¼	cup tomato paste
2	teaspoons thyme
2	teaspoons basil
1½	pounds fresh mushrooms, halved
¼	cup butter or margarine
¼	cup flour
¼	cup Cognac (optional)
	Salt, pepper

1. Sauté bacon in *8½-quart Sauce Pot* over medium heat 7 minutes or until cooked; remove with slotted spoon; reserve.

2. Dip chicken pieces in flour; shake off excess, sauté, a few pieces at a time, 8-10 minutes or until well browned; remove chicken; reserve; pour fat from pot.

3. Pour wine into pot; add onions, garlic, tomato paste, thyme, basil; bring just to boil; reduce heat to low; cover; simmer 30 minutes; add chicken; simmer 30 minutes longer; add mushrooms, bacon; continue simmering 20 minutes.

4. Melt butter in *7-inch Straight-Sided Fry Pan* over medium heat; add flour; cook 5 minutes or until mixture begins to brown, stirring constantly; add 2 cups wine mixture from pot; stir until smooth; return mixture to pot; bring back to simmer; add Cognac; season with salt, pepper to taste.

Makes 8-12 servings

CAPONATA
*A tempting salad of cold sautéed
vegetables; very easy to prepare.*

½	cup olive oil
2	cups chopped onions
3	large cloves garlic, minced
1	large eggplant (1″ cubes)
1	can (16-oz) tomatoes, chopped
3	tablespoons tomato paste
2	large zucchini, sliced
2	large green or red peppers (1″ cubes)
⅓	cup red wine vinegar
2	tablespoons basil
2	tablespoons oregano
2	tablespoons salt
	Pepper
2	cups thinly sliced celery
½	cup capers
½	cup sliced black olives
	Salt

1. Heat oil in *5-quart Dutch Oven* over medium heat; sauté onions until translucent; add garlic, eggplant; sauté until lightly browned.

2. Add tomatoes, tomato paste, zucchini, green pepper, vinegar, basil, oregano, salt, pepper to taste; cover; reduce heat to low; simmer 30 minutes; remove cover; simmer 10 minutes longer or until vegetables are tender; add celery, capers, olives; season with salt to taste; serve hot or cold.

Makes 2½ quarts

23

SEAFOOD PAELLA

Classic Spanish recipe; a spectacular burst of color and flavor.

- ½ cup olive oil
- ½ cup butter or margarine
- 1 cup chopped onions
- 3 cups raw long grain rice
- 6 cups (48-oz) canned chicken broth
- Pinch saffron (optional)
- 2 whole steamed lobsters (1½-lb each)
- 1 pound steamed mussels
- 1 pound steamed clams
- 1 pound cooked shrimp
- 1 pound cooked scallops
- ½ cup sliced pimiento
- 12 black pitted olives
- 2 cups peas (fresh or frozen)
- 12 artichoke hearts

1. Add oil, butter to *6-quart Electric Wok;* heat 3 minutes at 325°F.; stir-fry onions 6 minutes or until tender but not browned; push up sides; add rice; stir-fry 3-4 minutes or until kernels turn white; add chicken broth; bring to boil; reduce setting to 200°-225°F.; add saffron; cover; simmer 18-20 minutes or until rice is cooked.

2. Cut bodies of lobsters into 4 pieces; crack claws; add shellfish, vegetables; continue simmering until heated through.

Makes 12 servings

Variation:
May substitute 1 pound each cooked chicken and sausage pieces for part of seafood.

ROAST LAMB WITH LIMAS

Lima beans soak up the lamb juice for a delicious combination.

- 1 pound dry large lima beans
- 4 quarts water
- ¼ cup butter or margarine
- 2 pounds sliced onions
- 1 can (13¾-oz) beef broth
- 1 teaspoon salt
- ¼ teaspoon pepper
- 1 bay leaf
- 4 pound leg of lamb, shank removed
- 3 cloves garlic, thinly sliced
- 1 teaspoon rosemary
- Salt, pepper

1. Soak beans overnight in water; drain.

2. Bring water to boil in *8½-quart Sauce Pot* over medium-high heat; add beans; cover; reduce heat to low; simmer 45 minutes; drain; place in *15½ x 11 x 2-inch Bake & Roast Pan.*

3. Melt butter in *12-inch Chef Style Fry Pan* over medium heat; sauté onions 10-11 minutes or until lightly browned; add to beans in pan; combine broth, salt, pepper, bay leaf; pour over beans, onions; stir to blend; spread over bottom of pan.

4. Make small slits over top of lamb roast; insert garlic slices in slits; sprinkle with rosemary; season with salt, pepper to taste; place on bean-onion mixture; bake 1½ hours at 400°F. or until done; let stand 15 minutes before carving.

Makes 10-12 servings

VEGETABLE CURRY

A mélange of crunchy vegetables, steamed in layers.

- ¼ cup vegetable oil
- ¼ cup butter or margarine
- 2 cups chopped onions
- 3 cloves garlic, minced
- 2 tablespoons curry powder
- 1 teaspoon ginger
- 1 teaspoon cumin
- ¼ teaspoon cayenne pepper
- 1 can (1-lb) chick peas, drained
- 1 cup water
- 2 teaspoons salt
- Pinch pepper
- 6 cups cauliflowerettes
- 2 cups green beans (1″ pieces)
- 2 cups sliced carrots
- 2 cups sliced zucchini
- 1 green or red pepper (2″ strips)
- ½ cup raisins
- 2 medium tomatoes, diced
- 1 cup cashew nuts

1. Heat oil, butter in *5-quart Dutch Oven* over medium heat; add onions, garlic, curry powder, ginger, cumin, cayenne; sauté 5-7 minutes or until onions are translucent; stir in chick peas, water, salt, pepper.

2. Layer cauliflowerettes, green beans, carrots, zucchini, green pepper, raisins in pan; cover; cook over medium heat 30 minutes or until vegetables are tender; stir in tomatoes, cashews; serve over rice with yogurt, chutney, mandarin oranges, as desired.

Makes 8-10 servings

25

BRAISED CABBAGE
Sweetened by cooking in cider and tarragon—perfect with pork!

- **2 pounds cabbage, cored, quartered**
- **6 slices bacon (2″ pieces)**
- **1 teaspoon salt**
- **1 teaspoon tarragon**
- **½ teaspoon pepper**
- **1½ cups apple cider**

1. Pour 1 inch water into *5-quart Dutch Oven*; bring to boil over medium-high heat; add cabbage; cover; reduce heat to low; simmer 10 minutes; drain; coarsely chop cabbage.

2. Sauté bacon in *Au Gratin Pan* 7 minutes or until lightly browned; drain; make even layer in bottom of pan; top with chopped cabbage; sprinkle with salt, tarragon, pepper; pour cider over top; cover pan with aluminum foil; bake 1 hour at 375°F. or until cabbage is tender.

Makes 8-10 servings

GRATIN OF POTATOES
A delightful way to dress up potatoes for a party.

- **3 pounds potatoes, peeled (⅛″ slices)**
- **2½ cups milk**
- **3 teaspoons salt**
- **8 ounces shredded Swiss cheese**
- **6 tablespoons butter or margarine**
- **½ cup heavy cream**
- **½ teaspoon pepper**
- **½ teaspoon nutmeg**
- **Salt, pepper**

1. Place potatoes in *11-inch Chicken Fryer*; add milk; cover; simmer over low heat 15 minutes.

2. Spoon ⅓ the potatoes in *Au Gratin Pan*; sprinkle with 1 teaspoon salt, ½ cup cheese; dot with 2 tablespoons butter; repeat, making 2 more layers; pour cream over top; sprinkle with pepper, nutmeg.

3. Bake 45 minutes at 350°F. or until potatoes are tender, top is golden brown; season with salt, pepper to taste.

Makes 8-12 servings

NOODLE PILAF
Mozzarella cheese makes this an unusually tasty side dish.

- **¼ cup butter or margarine**
- **2 cups chopped onions**
- **1 pound fine egg noodles (3″ pieces)**
- **3 cups (24-oz) canned beef broth 🍲**
- **8 ounces shredded mozzarella cheese**
- **½ cup chopped green onions**
- **Salt, pepper**

1. Melt butter in *11-inch Chicken Fryer* over medium heat; sauté onions until lightly browned; add noodles; toss in butter 2-3 minutes.

2. Add broth; bring to boil; reduce heat to low; cover; simmer 6-8 minutes; add cheese, onions; simmer 2 minutes longer; season with salt, pepper to taste.

Makes 8 servings

26

DILL-CHEESE BREAD

The texture and color of this easy bread will dazzle your guests.

> 2   **loaves (1-lb each) frozen bread dough**
> 2   **teaspoons dried dill weed**
> 1½ **cups finely shredded Swiss cheese**

1. Thaw dough and knead following package directions, working in dill weed, cheese.

2. Divide in half; shape into 2 loaves; place in two *8½ x 4 x 3-inch Loaf Pans;* cover with towel; let rise 45 minutes or until doubled in bulk.

3. Bake 25-30 minutes at 400°F. or until golden brown; cool on wire rack.

Makes 2 loaves

AMARETTO SOUFFLE

The delicate taste of almond graces this feather-light frozen dessert.

> 6   **large whole eggs**
> 4   **large egg yolks**
>   **Pinch salt**
> ⅔ **cup sugar**
> ¼ **cup boiling water**
> 4   **teaspoons instant coffee powder**
> 1   **envelope unflavored gelatin**
> 1½ **cups heavy cream**
> ⅔ **cup amaretto liqueur**
>   **Unsweetened cocoa powder**

1. Make a waxed paper collar to fit *8-inch Round Cake Pan*, extending 2 inches above top of rim; secure with string and transparent tape.

2. With electric mixer, beat eggs, egg yolks, salt until frothy; gradually add sugar, continuing to beat 12-14 minutes or until mixture becomes thick.

3. Pour mixture into *5-quart Dutch Oven*; cook 6-6½ minutes over medium-low heat, stirring constantly with wooden spoon (using figure 8 motion) or until mixture is just warm (120°F.); remove from heat.

4. Combine water, coffee powder, gelatin; stir until completely dissolved; cool 4-5 minutes or until just warm; gently fold into egg mixture; cool to room temperature; chill 5 minutes.

5. Beat cream until soft peaks form; gradually beat in amaretto; gently fold into egg mixture; pour into prepared cake pan; freeze 8 hours or until set; when ready to serve, place in refrigerator 10 minutes, then gently remove waxed paper collar; sprinkle with cocoa powder; allow to stand at room temperature 15 minutes or until able to cut.

Makes 8-12 servings

Variations:
May substitute other liqueurs or combinations of liqueurs, such as créme de menthe, créme de cacao or orange-flavored liqueur.

27

LA PETITE FLEUR

A thin, rich, almost flourless cake that's sure to impress.

- **4 ounces unsweetened chocolate**
- **6 tablespoons butter**
- **6 tablespoons sugar**
- **3 eggs, separated**
- **2 tablespoons flour**
- **2 tablespoons sugar**

Glaze:
- **2 ounces unsweetened chocolate**
- **1 ounce semi-sweet chocolate**
- **2 tablespoons water**
- **2 tablespoons sugar**
- **2 tablespoons butter**

1. Break chocolate into *2-quart Sauce Pan;* melt over low heat, stirring occasionally; remove from heat; allow to stand 3 minutes; add in order the butter, sugar, egg yolks, flour, stirring well after each addition.

2. With electric mixer, beat egg whites until they hold their shape; add sugar; beat until peaks form; add ⅓ the egg whites to chocolate mixture, then fold in remaining egg whites.

3. Grease and flour *8-inch Round Cake Pan;* pour chocolate mixture into pan; bake 20 minutes at 350°F. or until toothpick comes out clean; allow to cool 20 minutes in pan, then invert onto wire rack; cool completely.

4. *To make glaze:* Break chocolate into *1-quart Sauce Pan;* add water, sugar; cook over low heat until chocolate is melted, stirring occasionally; stir in butter; pour glaze over cake; spread evenly; cool, then refrigerate until serving time.

Makes 8-12 servings

BRANDY SNAPS

Elegant rolled cookies, filled with flavored whipped cream.

- **⅔ cup ground almonds**
- **½ cup butter or margarine**
- **½ cup sugar**
- **2 tablespoons orange juice**
- **1 tablespoon flour**
- **1 cup heavy cream**
- **2 tablespoons orange-flavored liqueur**

1. Combine almonds, butter, sugar, orange juice, flour in *8-inch Chef Style Fry Pan;* cook over low heat 5-7 minutes or until butter melts, mixture thickens.

2. Drop by heaping teaspoonful onto ungreased *15½ x 12-inch Cookie Sheets* (6 per sheet); bake 6-7 minutes at 350°F. or until golden; let cool 1 minute; gently remove with spatula; roll around handle of wooden spoon; slip off gently; continue cooling on wire racks. (If cookies become difficult to remove from sheet, return to oven 1-2 minutes, or until soft.)

3. Beat cream with liqueur until stiff; place in barrel of *Super Shooter;* pipe into cooled cookies using decorator tip, filling one end, then the other; dust with confectioners sugar, as desired.

Makes 2½ dozen

28

BRANDY SNAPS

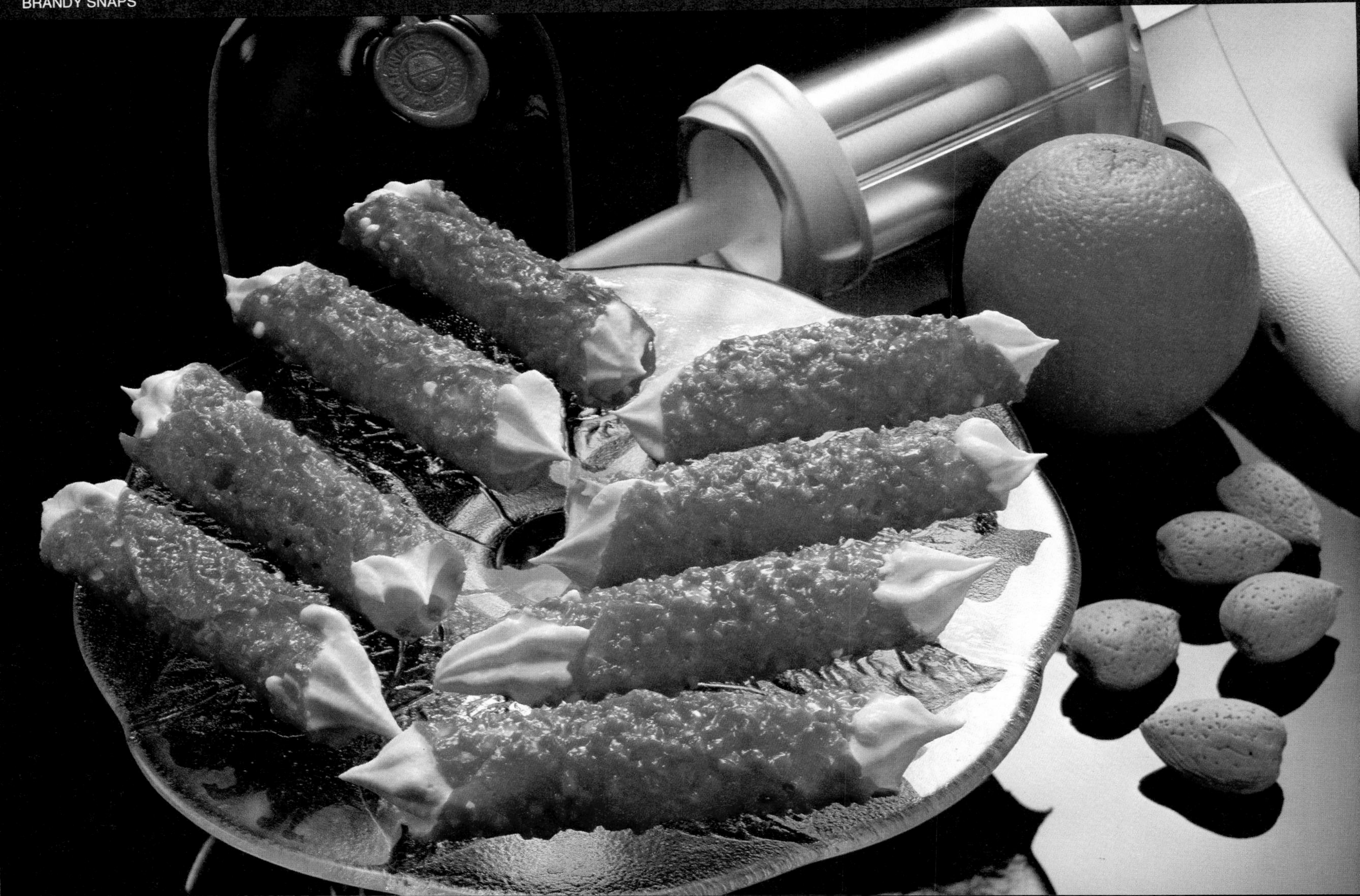

MENU SUGGESTIONS

gazpacho
SEAFOOD PAELLA
tossed green salad
white wine sangria
fresh fruit and cheese board

COLD WATERCRESS SOUP
ROAST LAMB WITH LIMAS
buttered baby carrots
red Burgundy
pecan pie

CHICKEN LIVER MOUSSE
COQ AU VIN
buttered noodles
tossed green salad
light red Burgundy, such as Beaujolais
French apple tart

VEGETABLE CURRY
sliced cucumbers with yogurt-mint dressing
pita bread
dry white wine
mandarin oranges and dates

MARINATED MUSHROOMS
roast beef
GRATIN OF POTATOES
peas with pearl onions
Zinfandel
LA PETITE FLEUR

CAPONATA
roast loin of pork
BRAISED CABBAGE
oven roasted potatoes
rosé wine
BRANDY SNAPS

melon with prosciutto
veal scallopini
NOODLE PILAF
hot spinach salad
young red Burgundy
AMARETTO SOUFFLE

sauerbraten
green beans with dill
DILL-CHEESE BREAD
German white wine
cheese cake

shrimp cocktail
grilled T-bone steak
GRATIN OF POTATOES
tomato onion salad
Italian Barolo
LA PETITE FLEUR (or fudge cake)

RAINY AFTERNOONS

"Boy, I hate rain! Tony and I were going to ride bikes to the park today."

"Why don't you ask him to come over anyway. You two can play checkers while I make some cookies."

The barometer may or may not affect people's moods, but it is a pretty sure bet that for most people bad weather is a great spoiler of plans, and few will venture to a park, beach or shopping center when the forecast is gloomy.

Even rain clouds have silver linings, however. "Cooking up a storm" can be a soothing exercise while it pours outside.

When you are stuck indoors, take a look through kitchen cabinets and chances are you will find enough ingredients to stir up some of the instant indoor gratification that will turn gray skies blue.

A rainy afternoon is the perfect time to make a soup that is a potpourri of all your leftovers. If your youngsters are disappointed when the weather turns bad, pick up their spirits with a big batch of baked goodies. Or, if you are by yourself, get out the popcorn popper and make a seasoned snack to munch while you watch the late afternoon vintage movie.

The recipes in this chapter were designed for ingredients that most people keep in their cupboards or freezers. Recipes include entrées and a good quota of gooey treats.

With a bit of cooking inspiration, neither snow, nor rain, nor ruined plans should keep anyone from making the sun shine—indoors—with something satisfying from the kitchen. ■

CHEESE POPCORN

A TV-watcher's favorite, with the added pizzazz of real cheese.

½ cup popcorn kernels
½ cup butter or margarine, melted
1 cup finely shredded Cheddar
   cheese
   Salt

1. Make popcorn in *Popcorn Pumper;* pour 4 quarts hot popcorn in large bowl.
2. Cool butter slightly; drizzle over popcorn; sprinkle with cheese, salt; toss well.

Makes 3 quarts

HOMEMADE POTATO CHIPS

Better than any store variety; you'll forget about bad weather.

2 pounds baking potatoes
1 quart vegetable oil
   Salt

1. Slice potatoes no more than ⅛-inch thick using vegetable slicer; soak 2 hours in cold water, changing water twice; drain; dry thoroughly.
2. Heat oil to 375°F. (on deep fat thermometer) in *11-inch Chicken Fryer* over medium-high heat.
3. Using slotted spoon, add potatoes to oil in small batches; fry until golden brown —adjust heat as necessary to maintain temperature; remove with slotted spoon; drain on paper towels; sprinkle with salt.

Makes 6-10 cups

GARDEN TERRINE

A dramatic way to use leftover vegetables.

1⅓ cups cooked, finely chopped
    red cabbage
1⅓ cups cooked, finely chopped
    spinach
1⅓ cups cooked, shredded carrots
2 packages (3-oz each) cream
    cheese
1 cup medium white sauce 🍳
    Salt, white pepper
3 cups fresh bread crumbs
3 tablespoons butter or
    margarine, melted

1. Place each vegetable in separate bowl; combine cream cheese, warm white sauce; season with salt, pepper; add ⅓ the sauce to each vegetable (about ⅔ cup); blend well; taste each vegetable mixture and correct seasonings.
2. Toss together bread crumbs, butter; press on bottom and sides of *8-inch Round Cake Pan.*
3. Assemble terrine by spreading cabbage mixture evenly over crumbs in bottom of pan; repeat with even layers of spinach, carrot mixtures.
4. Bake terrine 40-45 minutes at 400°F.; allow to stand at least 15 minutes; turn out onto serving plate; garnish with carrot tops or parsley, as desired; cut into wedges.

Makes 6-8 servings

ORIENTAL PORK TOASTS

A delicious appetizer for munching in front of the tube.

½ pound ground pork
2 small cloves garlic, minced
⅔ cup sliced green onions
¼ cup soy sauce
1 tablespoon sesame seeds
16 slices soft white bread
9 stalks celery
4 tablespoons butter or
   margarine, melted

1. Place pork, garlic in *10-inch Straight-Sided Fry Pan;* sauté over medium heat 8 minutes or until pork is cooked; add green onions, soy sauce; sauté 2 minutes longer; remove meat mixture with slotted spoon to food processor or blender; add sesame seeds; blend until smooth.
2. Trim crusts off bread; flatten each slice with rolling pin; spread about 1 tablespoon pork mixture on each bread slice; starting from long edge of bread, roll up jelly-roll fashion; refrigerate 1 hour.
3. Cut celery stalks into sixty-four 1-inch lengths; cut each bread roll into 4 equal pieces; allowing a 1-inch space from skewer handle, thread 4 celery pieces and 4 bread rolls alternately on each skewer; attach skewer guards.
4. Brush with butter; insert skewers into *Kabob-It* base; place glass cover over food; kabob 14-16 minutes or until nicely browned; repeat with remaining rolls; serve with mustard, as desired.

Makes 64

33

RILLETTE

A fancy name for "pork hash," served as a very smooth pâté.

- **3**   **pounds lean pork shoulder**
- **1**   **ham hock (optional)**
- **1**   **bay leaf**
- **2**   **teaspoons salt**
- **½**   **teaspoon pepper**
- **½**   **teaspoon thyme**
- **½**   **teaspoon coriander**
- **½**   **teaspoon allspice**
- **¼**   **teaspoon cinnamon**
- **½**   **cup butter or margarine, softened**

1. Place pork, ham hock, bay leaf, seasonings in *5-quart Dutch Oven*; cover with water; bring to boil over medium-high heat; reduce heat to low; simmer 2½-3 hours or until ½-inch liquid remains, meat is tender and falling off bone; cool to room temperature.

2. Discard ham hock, bay leaf; remove meat from bone; grind in food processor; add butter; process until well-blended, smooth; correct seasonings.

3. Place in terrine or small serving bowls; refrigerate 2-3 hours before serving; serve with melba toast, as desired.

Makes 4 cups

BLACK BEAN SOUP

Variation of the hearty Cuban recipe; perfect for a blustery day.

- **1½**   **cups dry black beans**
- **3**   **cups water**
- **4**   **slices bacon (¼" pieces)**
- **¾**   **cup diced celery**
- **½**   **cup chopped green onions**
- **⅓**   **cup chopped onions**
- **⅓**   **cup diced carrots**
- **6**   **cups (48-oz) canned beef broth** ♟
- **1**   **ham hock**
- **½**   **cup red wine**
- **½**   **cup tomato purée**
- **½**   **teaspoon oregano**
- **1**   **bouquet garni***
- **1**   **cup water**
- **½**   **cup raw rice**

1. Combine beans, water in *3-quart Sauce Pan*; bring to boil over medium-high heat; boil 2 minutes; remove from heat; allow to stand 1 hour; drain; set aside.

2. Sauté bacon in *8½-quart Sauce Pot* over medium heat until crisp; add celery, onions, carrots; sauté 8-10 minutes; add beans, broth, ham hock, wine, tomato purée, oregano.

3. Make bouquet garni; add to pot; bring to boil over medium-high heat; reduce heat to low; cover; simmer 2½ hours.

4. Add water, rice; continue cooking ½ hour or until rice is cooked, beans are tender; remove bouquet garni; discard; remove ham hock; cut meat from bone; return meat to pot.

Makes 2½ quarts

CROSTINI

A highly seasoned cheese appetizer — Italian-style.

- **½**   **pound Italian bread (2" slices)**
- **¼**   **cup olive oil**
- **¼**   **cup butter or margarine, melted**
- **1**   **can (2-oz) anchovy fillets**
- **8**   **ounces thinly sliced mozzarella cheese**
- **½**   **cup chopped fresh parsley**

1. Place bread slices in single layer across bottom of *11½ x 9 x 2-inch Bake & Roast Pan*.

2. Combine oil, butter, anchovies in blender container until smooth; carefully pour ½ mixture over bread.

3. Bake 5 minutes at 400°F. or until top of bread is toasted; turn bread; pour on remaining mixture; toast second side.

4. Place cheese on toast; bake 8 minutes or until cheese melts; sprinkle with parsley; serve at once.

Makes 6-8 servings

TIP:

***A BOUQUET GARNI is a selection of herbs used to season soups, stews and sauces. Parsley, thyme and bay leaves are usually the foundation. Other herbs may be added for specific flavor. They are tied together with a string or wrapped in cheesecloth, then placed directly into the cooking pot and removed before serving.**

For BLACK BEAN SOUP: tie together 10 peppercorns, 3 cloves garlic, 3 whole cloves and a bay leaf.

SPLIT-PEA SOUP

Warmer-upper for winter days; a good use for that leftover ham bone.

2	tablespoons butter or margarine
2	cups chopped onions
1	pound dried split peas
1½	cups peeled, cubed potatoes
1½	cups sliced carrots
1	ham bone
4½	quarts water
½	cup chopped fresh parsley
1	bay leaf
1	tablespoon thyme
	Salt, pepper
	Croutons

1. Melt butter in *8½-quart Sauce Pot* over medium heat; add onions; sauté 5 minutes; add split peas, potatoes, carrots, ham bone, water; bring to boil, skim off top occasionally.

2. Add parsley, bay leaf, thyme; reduce heat to low; cover; simmer 2½ hours or until peas are very tender.

3. Remove ham bone, bay leaf; ladle mixture into blender container, in several batches; blend on low speed until smooth; return to pot; season with salt, pepper to taste; heat to serving temperature; garnish with croutons.

Makes 3½ quarts

STORMY WEATHER SANDWICH

Vary this classic Reuben with ingredients from a rained-out picnic.

8	teaspoons prepared mustard
8	slices rye bread
8	ounces sliced Swiss cheese
1	pound sliced corned beef
1	cup sauerkraut
4	teaspoons butter or margarine

1. Spread 1 teaspoon mustard on each bread slice; on 4 of the slices, layer ½ cheese and corned beef; add sauerkraut, then remaining corned beef, cheese, in that order; top with remaining bread slices.

2. Melt butter on *Square Griddle* over medium heat; grill sandwiches 6-8 minutes per side or until golden brown.

Makes 4 servings

Variations:
- May substitute hot dogs for corned beef by slicing 8 hot dogs lengthwise into thin strips; sauté on preheated griddle until browned.
- May substitute coleslaw for sauerkraut.

POLYNESIAN POPCORN

Dried fruits add extra nourishment and extra chewiness.

½	cup popcorn kernels
1	cup butter or margarine
½	cup granulated sugar
½	cup light brown sugar
2	tablespoons water
1	tablespoon light corn syrup
1	teaspoon vanilla
1	cup dried pineapple chunks
1	cup chopped dried apricots
¾	cup cashew nuts
¾	cup flaked coconut

1. Make popcorn in *Popcorn Pumper;* measure 1 quart; store remaining for later use.

2. Melt butter in *3-quart Sauce Pan* over medium heat; stir in sugars; cook over low heat until mixture comes to a boil, stirring constantly; stir in water, corn syrup; continue to cook until mixture reaches 270°F. on candy thermometer, stirring frequently; remove from heat.

3. Stir in vanilla, 1 quart popcorn, pineapple, apricots, cashews, coconut; toss well to coat; spread onto greased *15½ x 12-inch Cookie Sheet;* cool 1 hour or until hardened; break into large pieces; store in air-tight container.

Makes about 2 quarts

STICKY BUNS

The traditional Philadelphia breakfast roll; a super-gooey treat.

2	loaves (1-lb each) frozen bread dough 🏆
½	cup butter or margarine, melted
1	cup dark brown sugar
½	cup light corn syrup
½	cup chopped pecans
¼	cup butter or margarine, melted
½	cup dark brown sugar
½	cup chopped pecans
½	cup light or dark raisins

1. Thaw dough and knead following package directions.

2. Melt butter in *2-quart Sauce Pan* over medium heat; stir in sugar, corn syrup; pour into bottom of *15½ x 11 x 2-inch Bake & Roast Pan;* sprinkle with pecans.

3. Roll each loaf into 14 x 9-inch rectangle; brush each rectangle with butter; sprinkle evenly with sugar, pecans, raisins; roll up to 9 inch long rolls.

4. Slice each roll into nine 1-inch pieces; arrange cut side up in the prepared pan; cover with towel; let rise 40 minutes or until dough reaches top of pan.

5. Bake 20-25 minutes at 375°F. or until golden brown; cool in pan 10 minutes; invert onto *15½ x 12-inch Cookie Sheet* to complete cooling.

Makes 18

VERMONT BREAD PUDDING

Sweetened with real maple syrup, and dotted with fresh blueberries.

½	cup butter or margarine
10	thin slices white bread, crusts removed, halved diagonally
6	eggs
⅓	cup pure maple syrup
3	cups milk
½	teaspoon vanilla
	Pinch salt
1½	cups fresh or frozen blueberries

1. Melt butter in *Au Gratin Pan* over medium heat; remove from heat; dip both sides of bread halves into butter; arrange along sides of pan and down center bottom; bake 10-12 minutes at 350°F. or until bread is lightly browned; remove pan from oven.

2. Combine eggs, maple syrup; beat well; gradually stir in milk; add vanilla, salt; blend well; add blueberries; pour into bread-lined pan; bake 30-35 minutes or until custard is just set; allow to cool 5 minutes before serving.

Makes 6-8 servings

HONEY CUSTARD

Traditional Alpine recipe, with an unusual nutty taste.

2½	cups milk
1	cup chopped walnuts
½	cup honey
3	whole eggs
3	egg yolks
	Pinch salt
	Walnuts, crystallized violets

1. Scald milk in *1-quart Sauce Pan* over medium heat; place walnuts in blender container with ½ scalded milk; blend until smooth; return to pan; let stand 1 hour.

2. Combine honey, eggs, egg yolks, salt; beat thoroughly; gradually add walnut-milk; blend; strain mixture into *8-inch Round Cake Pan.*

3. Pour 1 inch hot water into *11½ x 9 x 2-inch Bake & Roast Pan;* place cake pan into pan with water; cover large pan with aluminum foil; gently place in oven; bake 45-50 minutes at 350°F. or until metal knife comes out clean.

4. Remove from oven; remove foil; cool custard in water; remove from water; refrigerate at least 4 hours; invert custard onto serving plate; garnish with walnuts, crystallized violets.

Makes 6 servings

MOLASSES RAFTS

An old-fashioned favorite; quick and easy with today's tools.

- ½ **cup butter or margarine**
- ½ **cup sugar**
- ½ **cup molasses**
- 3½ **cups all purpose flour**
- 1 **teaspoon baking soda**
- 1 **teaspoon ginger**
- ½ **teaspoon cinnamon**
- ½ **teaspoon salt**
- ¼ **teaspoon cloves**
- ½ **cup water**

1. With electric mixer, beat butter thoroughly; add sugar, molasses; continue to beat until light, fluffy.

2. Lightly spoon flour into measuring cups; level off; thoroughly blend flour, baking soda, ginger, cinnamon, salt, cloves; add alternately with water in 3 additions; beat well after each addition.

3. Fill barrel of *Super Shooter* with ½ cookie dough; press strips of dough onto ungreased *15½ x 12-inch Cookie Sheets* using sawtoothed disc; score strips into 2-inch pieces; bake 10-11 minutes at 350°F. or until done; immediately cut strips along scored lines; remove from cookie sheets; repeat with remaining dough; cool on wire racks.

Makes 7-8 dozen

BLACK FOREST CAKE

An exotic combination of cherries, Kirsch and dark chocolate.

Batter:
- 4 **eggs**
- ½ **teaspoon vanilla**
- ⅔ **cup sugar**
- ⅓ **cup all purpose flour**
- ⅓ **cup unsweetened cocoa**
- 6 **tablespoons unsalted butter, melted**

Syrup:
- ¼ **cup sugar**
- ⅓ **cup cold water**
- 2 **tablespoons Kirsch**

Filling/Topping:
- 2 **cups heavy cream**
- 6 **tablespoons confectioners sugar**
- 2 **tablespoons Kirsch**
- 1 **can (16-oz) dark sweet cherries, drained**
- 1 **square semi-sweet chocolate, grated**

1. *To make batter:* With electric mixer at high speed, beat eggs, vanilla, sugar for 10 minutes or until thick, fluffy; combine flour, cocoa; add to egg mixture, a little at a time, folding gently to blend; stir in melted butter, 2 tablespoons at a time. (Do not overmix.)

2. Grease, flour two *8-inch Round Cake Pans;* pour batter evenly into pans; bake 10-15 minutes at 350°F. or until toothpick comes out clean; cool 5 minutes (layers will fall evenly as they cool so don't be alarmed); turn layers out onto waxed paper.

3. *To make syrup:* Combine water, sugar in *1-quart Sauce Pan;* bring to boil over medium heat; boil briskly 5 minutes; remove from heat; cool to lukewarm; stir in Kirsch.

4. Lightly pierce cake layers several times with sharp fork; sprinkle evenly with syrup; let stand 5 minutes.

5. *To make filling/topping:* With electric mixer, beat cream until slightly thickened; add sugar; continue to beat until peaks form; add Kirsch in thin stream, continuing to beat until blended.

6. *To assemble:* Pat cherries dry with paper towels; reserve 8 cherries for garnish; place one cake layer on serving plate; spread with ⅓ of whipped cream; arrange remaining cherries to within ½-inch of edge; top with second cake layer; spread remaining whipped cream over entire cake; garnish with reserved cherries; pat sides with grated chocolate, then sprinkle the rest on top; refrigerate until ready to serve.

Makes 6-8 servings

THE PLEASURE OF YOUR OWN COMPANY

"Now, that's one each of the china setting, water goblet, wine glass, damask napkin and placemat. Shall I gift wrap them?"

"No, thanks. They're for setting my own table this evening."

Dining alone can be one of life's most enjoyable small pleasures. Eating by yourself no longer necessarily means tuna fish or foil-wrapped hamburgers.

In fact, dining alone provides an opportunity to fulfill your most luxurious tastes or simplest wants. While a cut of the finest steak might upset the budget for a family of four, a single serving of tenderloin, cooked and seasoned to perfection, costs no more than a fast-food burger and fries.

Beyond bringing such treats as veal cutlet and fresh shrimp within range of the average pocketbook, dining alone gives you the opportunity to apply a heavy hand with favorite seasonings.

Without company, or other family members to offend, you can indulge in as much garlic, onions and cooked cabbage as will satisfy your palate.

Nor does the pleasure of self-indulgence stop with the choice of menu. Solo dining can mean abandoning the kitchen table for a bed-tray and your favorite old movie on the tube, or setting a dramatic table, complete with candlesticks, under the stars on the patio. Whatever the accoutrements, dining alone is a chance to treat yourself well.

All of the recipes in this chapter are designed to serve one person. They can be prepared in less than thirty minutes, and no matter how busy you may be, there's hardly an excuse for not taking advantage of a solitary dinner hour—and enjoying the pleasure of your own company! ∎

40

LEMON SOUP

*An example of how you can make
a complete meal with a bouillon cube.*

- ¾ **cup water**
- 1 **chicken bouillon cube**
- 1 **egg**
- 1 **tablespoon lemon juice**
  Pinch oregano
- ¼ **cup cooked rice**
  Salt, pepper

1. Heat water, bouillon cube in *1-quart Sauce Pan* until cube dissolves; remove from heat.

2. In small bowl, beat together egg, lemon juice, oregano; stir small amount of bouillon into egg mixture; blend, then return to pan.

3. Add rice; season with salt, pepper to taste; reheat without boiling; add more lemon juice, as desired.

Makes 1 serving

CHARLIE'S PAN-FRIED TROUT

A simple garnish makes this "everyday" fish look special.

- 1 **whole trout (½-lb), pan-dressed**
- 2 **tablespoons flour**
- ¼ **teaspoon sage**
- 1 **tablespoon butter or margarine**
- ¾ **cup thinly sliced mushrooms**
- 2 **tablespoons chopped green onions**
- 1 **teaspoon lemon juice**
  Salt, pepper
- 2 **slices lemon**

1. Rinse fish under cold running water; pat dry; open flat; combine flour, sage; coat fish with flour, shaking off excess.

2. Heat butter in *10-inch Chef Style Fry Pan* over medium heat until it sizzles; place fish in pan, skin side up; sauté 3-4 minutes or until golden brown.

3. Using large spatula, carefully turn fish over; sauté 5 minutes or until fish flakes; remove to serving plate.

4. Add mushrooms to pan; cook briefly, about 1 minute; add green onions, lemon juice; season with salt, pepper to taste; pour over fish; garnish with lemon slices, chives as desired.

Makes 1 serving

WELSH RAREBIT

A specialty served in the British Parliament, tasty and easy to make.

- ¼ **cup beer**
- ¼ **teaspoon paprika**
- ¼ **teaspoon dry mustard**
  Pinch cayenne pepper
- 1 **teaspoon butter or margarine**
- 1 **cup (4-oz) shredded Cheddar cheese**
- 1 **egg yolk**
- 1 **teaspoon Worcestershire sauce**
  Salt, pepper
- 2 **slices toasted bread***

1. Combine beer, paprika, mustard, cayenne in *1-quart Sauce Pan;* heat over medium heat; add butter, cheese; when cheese is melted, add egg yolk; continue to cook until mixture thickens. (Do not boil.)

2. Add Worcestershire; season with salt, pepper to taste; serve over toasted bread.

Makes 1 serving

*May substitute 6-ounce package frozen crabmeat, thawed and lightly sautéed in butter.

41

SHIRRED EGGS WITH CHEESE
Put this very simple entrée in the oven and put your feet up!

- 1   cup (4-oz) shredded Cheddar cheese
- 2   eggs
      Salt, pepper
- 1   teaspoon butter or margarine
- 1   teaspoon fresh snipped chives

1. Sprinkle ½ cup cheese in bottom of *8-inch Chef Style Fry Pan;* break eggs onto cheese; season with salt, pepper to taste; top with remaining cheese, covering eggs completely; dot with butter.
2. Bake 15-16 minutes at 350°F. or until cheese is melted, eggs set; sprinkle with chives before serving.

Makes 1 serving

Variation:
May substitute any good melting cheese.

TIP:

Wear-Ever cookware with plastic handles and knobs may be placed in the oven up to 350°F. without harming the material.

BAKED SOLE WITH ASPARAGUS
A perfect balance of two delicate flavors.

- 1   fillet of sole (½-lb)
- 6   thin asparagus spears, cooked
- ⅓   cup water
- 3   tablespoons chopped fresh tomatoes
- 1   tablespoon finely chopped green onions
- 1   tablespoon white wine
- ¼   teaspoon salt
      Pinch thyme
      Pepper
      Chopped fresh parsley

1. Place fish flat on cutting board; lay asparagus spears across wide end of fish, trimming to fit; roll up; secure with toothpicks.
2. Combine water, tomatoes, green onions, wine, salt, thyme, pepper in *8-inch Round Cake Pan;* place fish roll in pan; cover with aluminum foil.
3. Bake 15-18 minutes or until fish flakes; remove to serving plate; place pan over medium heat; simmer sauce 5 minutes or until ¼ cup remains; pour sauce over fish; sprinkle with chopped parsley.

Makes 1 serving

SCAMPI
A seafood favorite—lone diners needn't hold the garlic!

- 1   tablespoon olive oil
- 1   medium onion, sliced
- ½   cup green pepper strips
- ⅛   teaspoon minced garlic
- 6   large shrimp, shelled, deveined
- 2   tablespoons dry white wine
- 2   tablespoons canned tomato sauce
      Chopped fresh parsley
      Salt, pepper

1. Heat oil in *7-inch Straight-Sided Fry Pan* over medium heat; add onion, green pepper; sauté 8 minutes or until soft; add garlic; sauté 1 minute longer; remove vegetables with slotted spoon; reserve.
2. Add shrimp; sauté 3 minutes or until shrimp are barely firm to the touch; add wine, tomato sauce, reserved vegetables; cover; simmer 2 minutes or until heated through.
3. Sprinkle with parsley; season with salt, pepper to taste; serve at once.

Makes 1 serving

42

STEAK AU POIVRE

A classic recipe, very affordable for one.

- 1 **teaspoon black peppercorns**
- 6 **ounces beef tenderloin filet (1″ thick)**
- 1 **teaspoon vegetable oil**
- 2 **tablespoons canned beef broth**🍳
- 2 **tablespoons heavy cream**
- 4 **teaspoons Cognac**
  Salt
  Chopped fresh parsley

1. Place peppercorns between sheets of waxed paper on cutting board; using hammer, smash peppercorns into small pieces; press both sides of meat into peppercorns.

2. Heat oil in *8-inch Chef Style Fry Pan* over medium heat; sauté meat 4 minutes per side for rare, 5 minutes for medium, 6 minutes for well done.

3. Remove meat to serving plate; pour off fat; add broth, cream, Cognac; season with salt to taste; simmer 2 minutes; pour sauce over meat; sprinkle with chopped parsley.

Makes 1 serving

PORK CHOPS FLAMBE

When you feel like being dramatic, here's the fiery solution.

- ⅓ **cup fresh orange juice**
  Pinch nutmeg
  Pinch cinnamon
  Pinch ginger
- 1 **tablespoon vinegar**
- 2 **pork loin chops (¼″ thick), trimmed**
- 2 **tablespoons dark rum**
- 1 **tablespoon raisins**
  Flour
- 1 **teaspoon vegetable oil**
  Salt, pepper

1. Combine orange juice, nutmeg, cinnamon, ginger, vinegar; blend thoroughly; pour over pork chops; let stand 15 minutes, turning once.

2. In small bowl, combine rum, raisins; set aside.

3. Remove pork chops from marinade; reserve marinade; lightly dust chops with flour; heat oil in *8-inch Chef Style Fry Pan* over medium heat; sauté chops 5-7 minutes per side or until tender; remove to serving plate; season with salt, pepper to taste.

4. Pour fat from pan; add rum-raisin mixture; heat slightly over low heat, then ignite with match; simmer until flame goes out; add reserved marinade; simmer 2 minutes; pour sauce over pork chops.

Makes 1 serving

CORNISH HEN WITH TARRAGON

The ideal bird for one; secret to its tenderness is quick cooking.

- 1 **tablespoon butter or margarine**
- ½ **teaspoon tarragon**
- ½ **teaspoon lemon juice**
  Salt, pepper
- 1 **cornish game hen (about 1-lb)**
- ¼ **cup canned chicken broth**🍳
- 5 **cherry tomatoes**

1. Cream together butter, tarragon, lemon juice; season with salt, pepper to taste; spread mixture over exterior of hen and inside body cavity.

2. Place hen in *8-inch Round Cake Pan;* bake 25 minutes at 400°F. or until done. (To check for doneness, insert tip of knife behind leg; hen is done when juices run clear.)

3. Remove hen to serving plate; add broth, cherry tomatoes to pan; cook over medium heat 3-5 minutes or until tomatoes are barely soft; pour pan juices over hen; garnish with tomatoes.

Makes 1 serving

43

44

VERMICELLI OMELET

Sauté uncooked pasta for this crunchy variation on a staple entrée.

1   tablespoon olive oil
¼   cup uncooked vermicelli
2   eggs, slightly beaten
2   tablespoons milk
**   Pepper**
¼   cup grated Parmesan cheese
**   Tomato sauce** ♟

1. Heat oil in *8-inch Gourmet Style Fry Pan with metal handle* over medium heat; add vermicelli, broken into 2-inch pieces; sauté 3 minutes or until lightly browned, crispy.

2. Combine eggs, milk; season with pepper to taste; pour over vermicelli; cook until eggs are barely set; sprinkle with Parmesan.

3. With heavy mitt to protect hand, place pan under broiler; shake in circular motion to increase puffiness; broil 3-5 minutes or until top is lightly browned; serve with tomato sauce.

Makes 1 serving

Variations:
Add ¼ cup chopped cooked meat or vegetables.

DUXELLES CREPES

Rolled into crepes, this mushroom "hash" makes a delightful meal.

¾   cup pancake mix ♟
2   tablespoons butter or margarine
½   cup finely chopped onions
6   ounces finely chopped mushrooms
½   teaspoon salt
½   teaspoon sherry
1   tablespoon heavy cream
**   Pinch white pepper**
½   cup canned cheese sauce ♟

1. Prepare recipe for crepe batter following package directions; let stand 15 minutes.

2. Melt butter in *7-inch Straight-Sided Fry Pan* over medium heat; sauté onions 4-5 minutes or until soft; add mushrooms, salt; sauté 6-8 minutes or until all liquid is gone; add sherry, cream, pepper; cook additional 2 minutes.

3. Preheat *8-inch Gourmet Style Fry Pan with metal handle* over medium heat 2 minutes or until drops of water dance on dry pan surface; for each crepe, pour about 2 tablespoons batter into pan; immediately tilt pan to coat bottom evenly; cook 45 seconds or until top looks dry; turn; cook second side about 20 seconds. (Makes 12 crepes. ♟)

4. Place ½ duxelle mixture in center of 2 crepes; fold over into thirds; place in 8-inch pan with folded side down; bake 6 minutes at 350°F. or until crepes begin to brown; spoon on sauce; place under broiler 2-4 minutes or until sauce bubbles.

Makes 1 serving

CROQUE MADAME

You can substitute any sliced meat or cheese to make this quick meal.

2   slices bread, crusts removed
2   teaspoons butter or margarine
2   slices Monterey Jack cheese
1   slice Gouda cheese
2   slices cooked ham or turkey
½   teaspoon Dijon mustard

1. Spread one side of bread slices with butter; place one slice, butter side down; layer with cheeses, ham; spread with mustard; top with remaining bread slice, butter side up.

2. Place *8-inch Chef Style Fry Pan* over medium heat about 2 minutes or until drops of water dance on dry pan surface.

3. Place sandwich in pan; cook over medium-low heat 3-5 minutes or until golden brown on both sides.

Makes 1 serving

ZUCCHINI BASILICO

Grate zucchini right into the pan for a crunchy-textured side dish.

1	teaspoon butter or margarine
1	teaspoon olive oil
1	small clove garlic, minced
1	small zucchini, grated
¼	teaspoon basil
	Salt, pepper
1	teaspoon lemon juice

1. Heat butter, oil in *7-inch Straight-Sided Fry Pan* over medium heat; add garlic; sauté until light brown.
2. Add zucchini, basil; season with salt, pepper to taste; sauté 4 minutes or until zucchini is just cooked; sprinkle with lemon juice.

Makes 1 serving

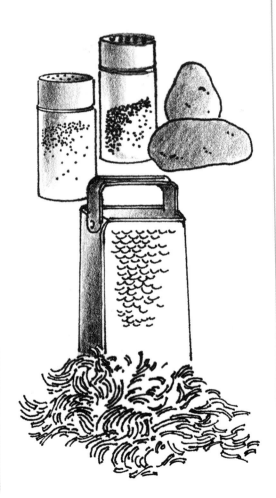

ROESTI POTATOES

The national potato dish of Switzerland— quick and delicious!

1	tablespoon butter or margarine
2	small raw potatoes, shredded
	Salt, pepper
1	teaspoon chopped green onions

1. Melt butter in *8-inch Chef Style Fry Pan* over medium heat until butter begins to foam; add potatoes; pack down with wooden spoon; cook 10 minutes.
2. Invert onto dinner plate; slide potatoes back into pan; cook second side another 10 minutes.
3. Slide out onto dinner plate; season with salt, pepper to taste; sprinkle with green onions.

Makes 1 serving

Variations:
May substitute apple sauce, sour cream or thin slices of cold meat for green onions.

45

BUTTERSCOTCH SAUCE
A great homemade topper for any dessert or late-night snack.

1 cup brown sugar
¼ cup light cream
2 tablespoons butter or margarine
2 tablespoons light corn syrup

1. Combine brown sugar, cream, butter, corn syrup in *1-quart Sauce Pan;* bring to boil over medium heat, stirring occasionally; remove from heat.

2. Serve warm over ice cream. (Leftover sauce may be refrigerated; to reheat, add 1 tablespoon water; cook over low heat, stirring occasionally.)

Makes 1 cup

Variation:
May add ⅓ cup any variety of chopped nuts.

POACHED PEAR
An easy way to make ordinary fruit into a very special dessert.

1 large pear, pared
¾ cup water
1 tablespoon sugar
½ teaspoon grated lemon peel
1 tablespoon apricot jam
⅛ teaspoon vanilla

1. Cut pear in half; remove core; place pear halves in *2-quart Sauce Pan* along with water, sugar, lemon peel; cover; bring to boil over medium heat; reduce heat to low; poach 7-10 minutes or until tender; remove pear halves.

2. Bring poaching liquid to boil; add apricot jam, vanilla; boil, uncovered, 5-7 minutes; pour sauce over pear; cool.

Makes 1 serving

QUANTIFYING RECIPES:

In most cases, recipes may be successfully doubled and tripled without major modifications. However, seasonings (salt, pepper, herbs and spices) may need adjusting. It is best to check seasonings during cooking.

This quantification rule does not apply to baked goods. Since precise measurements are critical, it is best to select a recipe with the adequate number of servings.

46

MENU SUGGESTIONS

48

WELSH RAREBIT
tomato and onion salad
beer or white table wine
ice cream with BUTTERSCOTCH SAUCE

CHARLIE'S PAN-FRIED TROUT
tossed green salad
French bread
dry white wine
fruit and cheese

STEAK AU POIVRE
new potatoes
watercress and orange salad
red wine
raspberry sherbet

CORNISH HEN WITH TARRAGON
parsley rice
broccoli spears with lemon juice
dry white or rosé wine
POACHED PEAR

cream of asparagus soup
DUXELLES CREPES
marinated sliced tomatoes with basil
dry white wine
fresh strawberries with sour cream
and brown sugar

VERMICELLI OMELET
ZUCCHINI BASILICO
white table wine
ice cream with FRUIT SAUCE
espresso

SCAMPI
rice
medium-dry white wine, such as
California Riesling
melon with lime and ginger

SHIRRED EGGS WITH CHEESE
ROESTI POTATOES
tossed green salad
dry white wine
broiled half grapefruit

PORK CHOPS FLAMBE
buttered noodles with caraway seeds
julienne of carrots
rosé wine
peppermint stick ice cream

Note: Since it may be difficult for one person to consume a bottle of wine at a single sitting, we recommend two strategies for singles. If you are a wine novice, and simply like a glass with your meals, buy inexpensive table wines. They can be recorked and will keep in the refrigerator (on their sides) for about a week.

If you're a wine lover, an economical way to have your favorite types and vintages with dinner is to purchase wine in half-bottles. These can also be recorked and stored in the refrigerator, but will be used up more quickly.

WINDING DOWN

"Ms. Abercrombie, we've got one more question for you. As president of your own company, what do you do for relaxation?"

"Well, after a really rough day, I like to go home, roll up my sleeves and make my own special omelet."

Coping with stress, one of the prevalent ailments of modern times, can be a problem. After a difficult day at home or at the office, many people seek an outlet for frustration and pent-up energy in competitive sports like tennis or racquetball.

Other busy people who never previously ventured into the kitchen in search of relaxation are finding that pounding a chicken cutlet into a tender meal can be as good a tension reliever as an early evening jog.

Cooking can be a relaxing exercise in two ways. First, by using recipes that demand a great deal of physical work —chopping, dicing, pounding, aggressive mixing—the day's tensions can be dissipated with a tasty result.

Second, a complex recipe that requires concentration will help erase thoughts of the day's hectic events.

Since cooking is also a creative exercise, the frustrations and tensions of the day can melt away with the feeling of accomplishment gained by producing a successful meal. The recipes in this chapter were designed for both kinds of "winding down" activities. Included are recipes that require physical labor, as well as those that demand care and attention for good results.

In a society that grows more competitive and demanding each day, everyone should find a resource for relaxation. The kitchen is a great place to start. ■

49

BROCCOLI SOUP

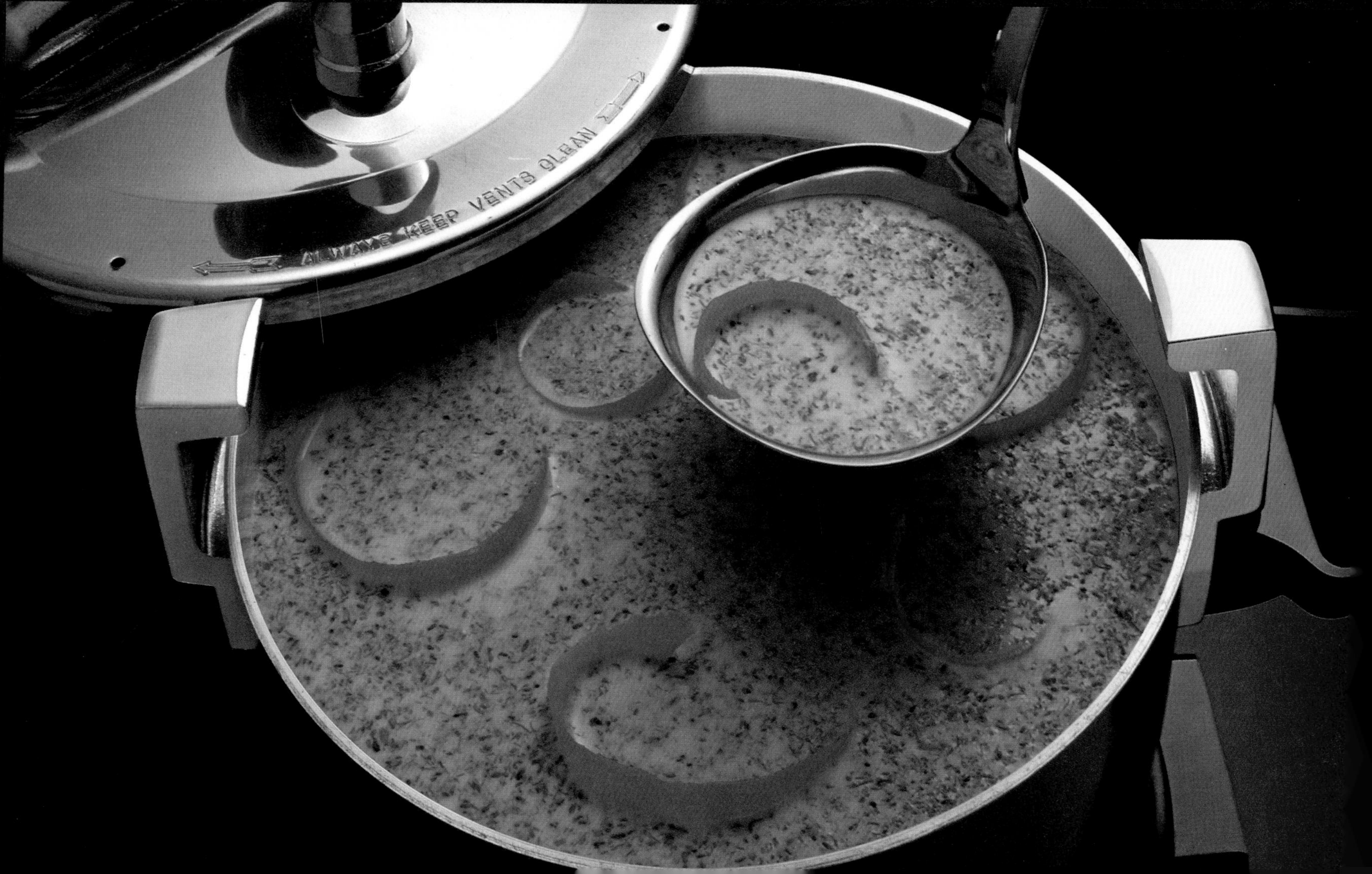

BROCCOLI SOUP
*A warm and soothing first course;
real comfort food.*

10	cups chopped fresh broccoli
1	large onion, chopped
3	cans (13¾-oz each) chicken broth
½	teaspoon tarragon
1	cup heavy cream
1	cup milk
	Salt

1. When preparing broccoli, cut 1 inch off bottom of stems; combine chopped broccoli, onions, chicken broth, tarragon in *6-quart Low Pressure Cooker/Fryer*; clamp on cover; bring up pressure on setting #9 (high heat); reduce to setting #2 (low heat); cook 8 minutes; turn off; reduce pressure.

2. Ladle mixture into blender container, in several batches; blend on low speed until mixture is just combined (specks of broccoli should remain); add cream, milk; season with salt to taste.

3. Return to cooker; warm soup on setting #2 (low heat); garnish with carrot curls, as desired. (When served cold, soup may require some additional seasoning.)

Makes 3 quarts

TUNA MELT
A quick, complete meal between two pieces of bread.

4	slices rye bread
4	teaspoons butter or margarine
1	can (7-oz) tuna, drained, flaked
3	tablespoons mayonnaise
1	tablespoon chopped celery
4	slices tomato
1	package (2-oz) alfalfa sprouts
2	leaves lettuce
2	ounces sliced Muenster cheese

1. Spread one side of bread slices with butter; combine tuna, mayonnaise, celery; blend well; spread on unbuttered side of two bread slices; add layers in order: tomato, sprouts, lettuce, cheese; top with remaining bread slices, butter side up.

2. Place *Square Griddle* over medium heat about 2 minutes or until drops of water dance on dry griddle surface; place sandwiches on griddle; cook over medium-low heat until golden brown on both sides.

Makes 2 servings

BEAN DIP
With taco chips, the ideal snack to accompany TV or a good book.

2	tablespoons butter or margarine
¼	cup chopped onions
1	tablespoon flour
1	can (8-oz) tomatoes, drained, chopped
2	tablespoons milk
1	can (20-oz) kidney beans, drained
½	cup shredded Monterey Jack cheese
2	tablespoons canned chili peppers, seeded, chopped
1	teaspoon salt
½	teaspoon cumin
	Taco chips

1. Melt butter in *2-quart Sauce Pan* over medium heat; sauté onions 3 minutes; add flour; continue cooking 3 minutes longer; add tomatoes, milk; reduce heat to low; simmer 8 minutes.

2. Mash kidney beans; add to tomato mixture along with cheese, chili peppers, salt, cumin; simmer 5 minutes longer or until cheese melts; serve hot with taco chips.

Makes 3 cups

51

BASIC OMELET

The anytime food; use our suggestions or your own favorite filling.

For Each Omelet:
- 1   **tablespoon cold water**
- ¼   **teaspoon salt**
-     **Pinch pepper**
- 3   **eggs**
- 1   **tablespoon butter or margarine**

1. Add water, salt, pepper to eggs; beat with whisk; melt butter in *8-inch Chef Style Fry Pan* over medium heat; pour in eggs; allow mixture to set around edges, then lift edge to allow uncooked egg mixture to slide underneath.

2. When omelet is set but still moist on top, add desired filling (see following recipes); spoon filling on top of omelet; tilt pan and flip ⅓ of omelet over filling, then slide omelet to lip of pan and flip onto serving plate.

Makes 1 serving

Variations:
May use 1 cup of one of the following fillings: any variety of shredded cheese, sautéed sliced mushrooms, chopped tomatoes, crisp diced bacon or Caponata (page 23).

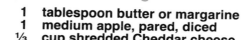

Apple Cheese Filling

- 1   **tablespoon butter or margarine**
- 1   **medium apple, pared, diced**
- ⅓   **cup shredded Cheddar cheese**
- 1   **teaspoon lemon juice**

1. Melt butter in *7-inch Straight-Sided Fry Pan* over medium heat; add apple; sauté until soft, about 3-5 minutes; add cheese, lemon juice; blend together; makes 1 serving.

Pear Ham Filling

- 1   **small pear, cored, sliced**
- 2   **slices smoked ham, chopped**
- 2   **tablespoons sour cream**

1. Combine pear, ham, sour cream; blend well; makes 1 serving.

SZECHUAN CHICKEN

The quick technique of stir-frying is a good energy releaser.

- 1   **large orange**
- 2   **whole chicken breasts, boned**
- ½   **cup orange juice**
- 1   **tablespoon soy sauce**
- 1   **tablespoon sherry**
- 1   **tablespoon cornstarch**
- ¼   **teaspoon crushed red pepper**
- ¼   **teaspoon ginger**
- 2   **tablespoons vegetable oil**
- 1   **cup sliced green onions (2″ pieces)**
- ½   **cup sliced water chestnuts**

1. Peel orange making 1½-inch wide strips; cut strips into 1-inch pieces; place peel in *8-inch Round Cake Pan*; bake 30 minutes at 200°F.; remove from oven; reserve.

2. Remove skin from chicken; cut meat into 1½-inch pieces; combine orange juice, soy sauce, sherry, cornstarch, red pepper, ginger; blend well; set aside.

3. Add oil to *6-quart Electric Wok*; preheat at 325°F. about 2 minutes; add chicken pieces; stir-fry 2-3 minutes or until chicken turns white; make well in center.

4. Add onions, water chestnuts; stir-fry about 1 minute; make well in center; stir sauce, then add to center of wok; bring to boil without stirring, about 1 minute; cook additional 1 minute or until thickened; stir rest of ingredients with sauce; sprinkle with orange peel before serving.

Makes 4 servings

CHICKEN PICCATA

Pound those chicken breasts, and forget today's troubles!

2	whole chicken breasts, boned
¼	cup flour
1	teaspoon salt
½	teaspoon pepper
3	tablespoons butter or margarine
2	tablespoons olive oil
1	large clove garlic
½	cup white wine
2	tablespoons lemon juice
¼	cup chopped fresh parsley
	Lemon slices

1. Remove skin from chicken; place chicken pieces between several thicknesses of waxed paper; pound until thin; combine flour, salt, pepper; sprinkle over chicken; shake off excess.

2. Heat butter, oil in *10-inch Straight-Sided Fry Pan* over medium heat; sauté garlic until brown; remove; add chicken; sauté 2 minutes per side or until nicely browned; add wine, lemon juice; reduce heat to low; simmer 3 minutes; serve sauce over chicken; sprinkle with parsley; garnish with lemon slices.

Makes 4 servings

CINNAMON BREAD

The goodness of homemade bread, without spending hours.

2	loaves (1-lb each) frozen bread dough
2	tablespoons butter or margarine, melted
½	cup sugar
2	teaspoons cinnamon
⅔	cup raisins

1. Thaw dough and knead following package directions; roll each loaf into 12 x 9-inch rectangle.

2. Brush butter on each rectangle; combine sugar, cinnamon; sprinkle over dough; top with raisins; roll up dough starting from short side; place rolls in two *8½ x 4 x 3-inch Loaf Pans*; cover with towel; let rise 45 minutes or until doubled in bulk.

3. Bake 40 minutes at 375°F. or until golden brown; cool on wire rack.

Makes 2 loaves

DONNA'S SANDWICH COOKIES

Working with dough is a great tension reliever.

1	cup butter or margarine
1	teaspoon vanilla
1	cup confectioners sugar
1½	cups all purpose flour
¼	teaspoon mace
5	squares semi-sweet chocolate, melted

1. With electric mixer, beat butter, vanilla thoroughly; add sugar gradually, continuing to beat until light, fluffy; thoroughly blend flour, mace; add to butter mixture, beating until smooth; refrigerate 45 minutes.

2. Form dough into forty ¾-inch balls (2 teaspoons each); place on ungreased *15½ x 12-inch Cookie Sheets,* allowing 12 balls per sheet; flatten cookies with bottom of glass.

3. Bake 12-15 minutes at 350°F. or until golden brown; remove to wire rack to cool; spread melted chocolate on bottom of ½ the cookies; top with remaining cookies; press together gently.

Makes 1¾ dozen

53

SPRITZ COOKIES

A classic butter cookie, quick and easy to prepare.

½   **cup butter or margarine**
¼   **cup vegetable shortening**
¾   **cup sugar**
1   **large egg**
2   **teaspoons vanilla**
2   **cups all purpose flour**
¼   **teaspoon baking powder**
¼   **teaspoon salt**

1. With electric mixer, beat butter, shortening thoroughly; add sugar gradually, continuing to beat about 5 minutes until light, fluffy; add egg, vanilla; beat well.

2. Lightly spoon flour into measuring cup; level off; thoroughly blend flour, baking powder, salt; add in 3 additions; mix well after each addition; dough will be stiff.

3. Fill barrel of *Super Shooter* with ½ cookie dough; press out cookies onto ungreased *15½ x 12-inch Cookie Sheets* using desired disc, spacing cookies 2 inches apart on sheets.

4. Bake 10-12 minutes at 375°F. or until just starting to turn light golden around edges, being careful not to overbake; gently remove to wire rack.

Makes 6-7 dozen

BLONDIES

A light-colored "brownie" with the traditional satisfying chewiness.

½   **cup butter or margarine**
2   **cups light brown sugar**
2   **teaspoons vanilla**
2   **eggs**
2   **cups all purpose flour**
2   **teaspoons baking powder**
1   **teaspoon salt**
1   **cup semi-sweet chocolate pieces**

1. With electric mixer, beat butter thoroughly; gradually add sugar; continue to beat until light, fluffy; add vanilla, eggs; beat well; add flour, baking powder, salt; beat thoroughly; stir in chocolate pieces.

2. Pour batter into greased and floured *11½ x 9 x 2-inch Bake & Roast Pan*; spread evenly; bake 22-25 minutes at 350°F. or until done; cool; cut into pieces.

Makes 2 dozen

PEANUT-RAISIN BRITTLE

A chewy twist on the traditional treat.

1   **cup sugar**
½   **cup light corn syrup**
¼   **cup water**
½   **teaspoon salt**
1   **tablespoon butter or margarine**
½   **teaspoon vanilla**
¼   **teaspoon baking soda**
1   **cup peanuts**
½   **cup light or dark raisins**

1. Combine sugar, corn syrup, water, salt in *2-quart Sauce Pan*; bring to boil over medium heat, stirring until sugar dissolves; cook, stirring frequently, until temperature reaches 285°F. on candy thermometer; remove from heat.

2. Stir in butter, vanilla, baking soda, peanuts, raisins; pour at once onto ungreased *15½ x 12-inch Cookie Sheet*; with 2 forks, lift and pull mixture into 14 x 12-inch rectangle; cool; break into pieces.

Makes 1 pound

54

PEANUT-RAISIN BRITTLE

CHOCOLATE KISSES
A super treat for giving—and receiving!

1 package (12-oz) semi-sweet chocolate pieces
1 can (14-oz) sweetened condensed milk
   Pinch salt
¼ cup crème de menthe*

1. Combine chocolate pieces, condensed milk, salt in *3-quart Sauce Pan*; cook over medium-low heat until melted, stirring frequently; stir in crème de menthe; beat until smooth.

2. Pour mixture into bowl; cool slightly; cover top of mixture with plastic wrap; let stand overnight at room temperature.

3. Fill barrel of *Super Shooter* with ½ the chocolate mixture; make mounds 1 x ¾-inch onto waxed paper using decorator tip; repeat with remaining mixture; allow to stand several hours or overnight until kisses can be easily removed from waxed paper.

Makes 7 dozen

*May substitute 1 teaspoon peppermint extract.

LIZA'S CHOCOLATE SAUCE
The ultimate for chocolate fanatics.

1 cup sugar
½ cup light cream
4 squares unsweetened chocolate
½ cup butter or margarine
2 egg yolks, slightly beaten
1 teaspoon vanilla

1. Combine sugar, cream in *2-quart Sauce Pan;* cook over medium heat, stirring constantly, 6-7 minutes or until sugar dissolves, mixture comes to boil; add chocolate, butter; continue to cook and stir until smooth, melted; remove from heat.

2. Gradually add ½ cup chocolate mixture to egg yolks, stirring constantly; pour back into remaining chocolate mixture; cook over low heat, stirring constantly, 3 minutes; remove from heat; stir in vanilla; serve hot over ice cream or pound cake, as desired.

Makes 2 cups

56

Sundays

"What are you cooking, Dad?"

"Pancakes and sausage."

"Oh, boy, that's why I love Sundays. No cold cereal!"

Sunday, traditionally the weekly day of rest, has evolved as a day with special meaning to nearly everyone. It is a day when families gather 'round the table for a special breakfast or dinner together. Many armchair enthusiasts spend whole Sunday afternoons in front of the television, "tuned in" to special snacks and seasonal team sports. And it is a day almost everyone associates with good aromas from the kitchen.

Since there are no school bus schedules, shopping trips or heavy chores, cooking can be a fulfilling way to spend a Sunday, baking treats to last all week long, or preparing meals that are more special than "everyday." Everyone is more relaxed than usual, too, making Sunday an opportune time to experiment with new recipes.

If you are not the ambitious sort, however, there is no need to make a grand production in the kitchen. Hot soups and sandwiches, which are recipes that do not take a lot of watching and concentration, can allow you the freedom to read the entire Sunday paper or watch all your favorite games on TV.

The recipes in this chapter were designed to meet the various possibilities that Sundays afford: delicious dessert treats, simple snacks, easy supper recipes and entrées for that special Sunday breakfast, brunch or dinner.

No matter how you decide to spend your day of rest, Sunday cooking can produce pleasurable, interesting—even exciting—results. ■

BEEF-BARLEY SOUP

Add a salad, and this hearty soup makes a complete meal.

- ¼ cup butter or margarine
- 2 cups chopped onions
- 2 pounds lean chuck (1″ cubes)
- 4 quarts water
- 6 beef bouillon cubes
- 1⅓ cups medium pearl barley (8-oz)
- 2 cups sliced carrots
- 2 cups chopped onions
- 2 cups chopped celery
  Salt, pepper
  Chopped fresh parsley

1. Melt butter in *8½-quart Sauce Pot* over medium heat; sauté onions 5 minutes; add meat; sauté 5-7 minutes or until lightly browned, tossing occasionally.

2. Add water, bouillon cubes; bring to boil over medium-high heat; cover; reduce heat to low; simmer 45 minutes; add barley; cook 30 minutes; add carrots, onions, celery; cook 30 minutes longer or until done; season with salt, pepper to taste; garnish with chopped parsley.

Makes 4 quarts

FARMER'S OMELET

A one-pan meal with a delicious smoky taste; great for brunch.

- 1 tablespoon bacon drippings
- 2 cups cooked, sliced potatoes
- 1 medium onion, thinly sliced
- 1 cup cooked, diced bacon
- 7 eggs
- 2 tablespoons milk
- 1 teaspoon salt
  Pinch pepper
  Pinch nutmeg
  Parsley sprigs

1. Heat bacon drippings in *10-inch Straight-Sided Fry Pan* over medium heat; sauté potatoes, onions about 15-20 minutes or until brown on all sides, turning occasionally; sprinkle bacon on top.

2. Beat together eggs, milk, salt, pepper, nutmeg; pour over potato mixture; cover; cook about 10 minutes or until eggs are set, omelet puffy around edges. (During cooking, occasionally remove cover; tilt pan; slip plastic spatula around sides of pan to allow uncooked egg mixture to flow underneath.)

3. Serve from pan or gently slide onto serving plate; garnish with parsley; cut in pie-shaped wedges.

Makes 6-8 servings

TOAD-IN-THE-HOLE

A giant popover stuffed with sausage.

- 2 eggs (room temperature)
- 1 cup all purpose flour
- ½ teaspoon salt
- 1 cup milk (room temperature)
- 6 sausage links
  Maple syrup

1. In small bowl, beat eggs until frothy; in large bowl combine flour, salt; make well in center; beat in eggs, milk until large bubbles show on surface; cover bowl; refrigerate 1 hour.

2. Preheat *10-inch Gourmet Style Fry Pan with metal handle* over medium heat 2 minutes or until drops of water dance on dry pan surface; sauté sausages 8 minutes or until browned; remove from heat; pour off all but 2 tablespoons fat.

3. Beat batter again; pour immediately into heated pan over sausages; bake 20 minutes at 425°F., then reduce to 375°F.; continue baking 10 minutes longer or until pudding has risen, is golden brown; serve immediately with maple syrup.

Makes 3-4 servings

59

60

STUFFED PORK ROAST

A savory prune stuffing makes this a very special Sunday dinner.

2	tablespoons butter or margarine
¼	cup chopped onions
¼	cup chopped celery
6	slices raisin bread, crumbled
6	large pitted prunes, halved
¼	cup fresh orange juice
1	egg
1	teaspoon salt
½	teaspoon pepper
¼	teaspoon rosemary
3	pounds pork roast, boned, rolled
1	large clove garlic, thinly sliced Salt, pepper
8	small potatoes, peeled, halved

1. Melt butter in *10-inch Straight-Sided Fry Pan* over medium heat; sauté onions, celery until soft; remove from heat; add crumbs, prunes, orange juice, egg, salt, pepper, rosemary; blend thoroughly.

2. Remove string from roast; unroll; spread stuffing on inside of roast; roll; tie with heavy string; make several small slits on outside of roast; insert garlic slices in slits; sprinkle with salt, pepper.

3. Place roast in *15½ x 11 x 2-inch Bake & Roast Pan*; bake 1 hour at 325°F.; arrange potatoes around roast; bake 1 hour longer or until meat and potatoes are done (turn potatoes several times during cooking to allow even browning); let stand 10-15 minutes before serving.

Makes 6-8 servings

REUBIN'S CORNED BEEF

A most intriguing braised-in-beer version.

4	pounds corned beef brisket
2	bottles stout ale (12-oz each)
2	bottles regular beer (12-oz each)
¼	cup Dijon mustard
2	tablespoons brown sugar
2	tablespoons honey Sauerkraut

1. Place brisket in *5-quart Dutch Oven*; pour stout ale, beer over meat; bring to boil over medium-high heat; reduce heat to low; cover; simmer 40 minutes per pound (about 2¾ hours) or until done, turning once halfway through cooking.

2. Allow meat to cool in cooking liquid; remove meat; discard liquid; place meat in *11½ x 9 x 2-inch Bake & Roast Pan*.

3. Combine mustard, sugar, honey; brush on meat; bake 20 minutes at 375°F. or until nicely glazed; thinly slice meat; serve with sauerkraut.

Makes 10-12 servings

TIP:

Stout ale is a robust and highly flavored beer made from roasted grains. The most common brand available in the United States is Guinness.

BUBBLE-AND-SQUEAK

Traditional British meat and vegetable hash; an easy Sunday supper.

½	pound bulk sausage
½	cup chopped onions
1	pound boiled potatoes, coarsely mashed
1	pound shredded cabbage, cooked
2	teaspoons prepared horseradish
1	teaspoon salt

1. Break sausage into bite-size pieces; place in *12-inch Chef Style Fry Pan*; sauté over medium heat until brown; remove sausage with slotted spoon; drain on paper towels; pour off all but 2 tablespoons fat.

2. Add onions; sauté until tender; return sausage to pan; add potatoes, cabbage, horseradish, salt; stir to blend, then gently pat mixture down in pan.

3. Cook 20 minutes, occasionally turning with pancake turner, until golden brown; spoon out of pan to serve.

Makes 4 servings

STIR-FRIED SALAD
A crunchy mélange of good things from the vegetable garden.

3	tablespoons sesame oil
2	large onions, thinly sliced
6	tablespoons vinegar
4	teaspoons lemon juice
1	teaspoon salt
1	teaspoon Dijon mustard
12	green onions (½" slices)
1	cup cauliflowerettes
3	carrots, diagonally sliced
2	stalks celery, diagonally sliced
3	small zucchini, grated
2	red peppers, cut in strips
2	tomatoes, cut in wedges
1	cup bean sprouts
1	large avocado, peeled, sliced
1	cup raw cashew nuts

1. Add oil to *6-quart Electric Wok*; preheat at 325°F. about 2 minutes; add onions; stir-fry 3-4 minutes or until translucent; combine vinegar, lemon juice, salt, mustard; add to wok; cook 2 minutes.

2. Add green onions, cauliflowerettes, carrots, celery, zucchini, red pepper; cover; cook 2 minutes; turn probe off; add tomatoes, sprouts, avocado, nuts; toss together.

Makes 8-10 servings

BERRY TRIFLE
Layers of pudding and fresh berries make plain pound cake special.

3	cups sliced fresh peaches
2	tablespoons sugar
1	cup fresh strawberry halves
4	containers (4-oz each) refrigerated vanilla pudding
¼	teaspoon almond extract
4	teaspoons sherry
	Pinch salt
1	pound cake, thinly sliced (1-lb)
½	cup seedless raspberry preserves, melted
2	cups whipped cream
2	tablespoons sugar
2	teaspoons sherry

1. Place peaches in bowl; sprinkle with sugar; refrigerate peaches, strawberries; flavor pudding with almond extract, sherry, salt.

2. Arrange slices of pound cake in bottom, along sides of 2-quart serving dish; pour raspberry preserves over bottom; make layers as follows—sliced peaches, ½ pudding, remaining pound cake slices, remaining pudding; arrange strawberries over top; refrigerate 2 hours or overnight.

3. Flavor whipped cream with sugar, sherry; place in barrel of *Super Shooter*; decorate top of trifle using decorator tip; garnish with fresh fruit, as desired.

Makes 6-8 servings

Variation:
A variety of fruits may be substituted depending on time of year.

APPLE-COOKIE CRUMBLE
A truly distinctive variation on traditional apple crisp.

8	cups thinly sliced apples (4-lb)
½	cup raisins
½	cup chopped pecans
1	tablespoon grated lemon peel
⅓	cup honey
2	tablespoons apple brandy (optional)
1	cup amaretto cookie crumbs (20 cookies)
2	tablespoons butter or margarine
	Whipped cream, sour cream

1. Combine apples, raisins, pecans, lemon peel, honey, brandy; toss well; pour into *Au Gratin Pan*; spread evenly; sprinkle with cookie crumbs; dot with butter.

2. Bake 40-45 minutes at 350°F. or until apples are tender; serve warm or cold; garnish with whipped cream, sour cream, as desired.

Makes 8 servings

Variations:
May substitute crushed macaroon or oatmeal cookies.

61

HAM CREPES

Flavored with a touch of sherry; perfect for an elegant brunch.

- ¾ **cup pancake mix** 👨‍🍳
- 1 **tablespoon butter or margarine**
- 1 **pound sliced ham (thin strips)**
- 2 **tablespoons Madeira or dry sherry**
- 1 **cup heavy cream**
- ¼ **teaspoon pepper**
- ⅓ **cup sliced green onions**

1. Prepare recipe for crepe batter following package directions; let stand 10-20 minutes.

2. Melt butter in *7-inch Straight-Sided Fry Pan* over medium heat; sauté ham 2-3 minutes or until lightly browned; remove with slotted spoon; keep warm; add Madeira, cream to pan; simmer sauce 6-8 minutes or until ½ remains; add pepper, green onions; simmer 1 minute.

3. Preheat *8-inch Chef Style Fry Pan* over medium heat 2 minutes or until drops of water dance on dry pan surface; for each crepe, pour about 2 tablespoons batter into pan; immediately tilt pan to coat bottom evenly; cook 45 seconds or until top looks dry; turn; cook second side about 20 seconds. (Makes 12 crepes.)

4. Place ham in center of each crepe; fold over into thirds; spoon sauce over top.

Makes 4 servings

FRENCH TOAST

A Sunday favorite, made continental style with crusty bread.

- 8 **eggs**
- 1 **cup milk**
- 1 **tablespoon grated orange peel**
- 1 **teaspoon cinnamon**
- 12 **French bread slices (¾" thick)**

1. Combine eggs, milk, orange peel, cinnamon; beat thoroughly; pour into shallow pan or plate; place bread slices, a few at a time, into egg mixture; let soak 1-2 minutes, turning to coat both sides.

2. Place *Double Griddle* over two units of range; preheat over medium heat about 2 minutes or until drops of water dance on dry griddle surface.

3. Place ½ bread slices onto ungreased griddle; cook about 2-3 minutes each side or until browned; repeat with remaining slices; serve with butter, honey, confectioners sugar or maple syrup, as desired.

Makes 4-6 servings

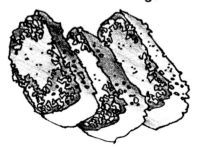

BUTTERMILK PANCAKES

Fresh buttermilk adds extra richness to the batter.

- 1½ **cups all purpose flour**
- ½ **cup vacuum packed wheat germ**
- 2 **tablespoons baking powder**
- 4 **teaspoons granulated sugar**
- 2 **teaspoons light brown sugar**
- 1 **teaspoon salt**
- 6 **eggs, well beaten**
- 1 **cup buttermilk**
- ¼ **cup butter or margarine, melted**

1. Combine flour, wheat germ, baking powder, sugars, salt; blend well; add to eggs; beat until smooth; stir in buttermilk, butter until combined.

2. Preheat *Double Griddle* over medium heat 2 minutes or until drops of water dance on dry griddle surface.

3. Pour batter by ¼ cupful onto ungreased griddle (6 at a time); turn cakes after 2 minutes or when bubbles break on top; continue cooking about 1 minute or until cakes are golden brown—adjust heat as needed. (For maximum flavor, allow batter to stand covered several hours before using.)

Makes 16

CRAN-ORANGE COFFEECAKE

Like love and marriage, Sundays and coffeecake go together.

- ½ cup milk
- ½ cup sugar
- ¼ cup butter or margarine
- 1½ teaspoons salt
- ½ cup water (105° - 115°F.)
- 2 packages active dry yeast
- 2 eggs, slightly beaten
- 5 cups all purpose flour
- 1 cup fresh cranberries*, ground
- 1 small orange, ground
- ¾ cup dark brown sugar
- 1 egg yolk
- 2 tablespoons milk
- ¼ cup dark brown sugar

1. Scald milk in *1-quart Sauce Pan* over low heat; add sugar, butter, salt; cool to lukewarm.

2. Measure water into large bowl; add yeast; stir until dissolved; add milk mixture, eggs, 3 cups flour; beat with wooden spoon until smooth; stir in additional flour to make stiff dough.

3. Turn out onto lightly floured board; knead 8-10 minutes or until smooth, elastic; place in greased bowl; cover with towel; let rise 45 minutes or until doubled in bulk.

4. Combine cranberries, orange, brown sugar in same pan; bring to boil over medium heat; reduce heat to low; simmer 5 minutes; cool.

5. Punch dough down until all air is forced out; divide dough in half; roll each piece into 13 x 9-inch rectangle; spread ½ cranberry-orange filling on ⅔ of each rectangle; fold unspread dough over ½ of spread dough, then fold again to form 3 layers of dough (2 with filling); seal edges.

6. Place dough on two *15½ x 12-inch Cookie Sheets*; using scissors, cut 8 strips along length of each rectangle to within 1 inch of opposite side; separate strips slightly; twist to show filling; cover with towel; let rise 45 minutes or until doubled in bulk.

7. Combine egg yolk, milk; brush over dough; sprinkle with brown sugar; bake 20-25 minutes at 350°F. or until golden brown; cool on wire racks.

Makes 2 coffeecakes

*May use frozen cranberries; or substitute 1½ cups prepared cran-orange relish for filling recipe.

CINNAMON DOUGHNUTS

Why go to the bakery? It's fun to make these, more fun to eat them.

- 2 eggs (room temperature)
- 1 cup sugar
- 1 cup milk (room temperature)
- ¼ cup butter or margarine, melted
- 1 teaspoon grated lemon peel
- 4 cups all purpose flour
- 4 teaspoons baking powder
- ½ teaspoon salt
- 2½ quarts vegetable oil
- ⅓ cup sugar
- 1 teaspoon cinnamon

1. Beat eggs; gradually add sugar, continuing to beat; stir in milk, butter, lemon peel.

2. Thoroughly blend together flour, baking powder, salt; add to egg mixture in 3 additions; mix well after each addition; refrigerate 15 minutes.

3. Roll dough out on lightly floured board to ½-inch thickness; cut with floured 2½-inch doughnut cutter.

4. Preheat oil to 375°F. (on deep fat thermometer) in *5-quart Dutch Oven* over medium-high heat; fry doughnuts, a few at a time, about 1½ minutes per side or until golden brown—adjust heat as necessary to maintain temperature; remove with slotted spoon; drain on paper towels.

5. Combine sugar, cinnamon; sprinkle over doughnuts while warm.

Makes about 1½ dozen

FLAKY FRIED PIES
A tasty finger food with many ethnic variations.

2	cups all purpose flour
½	teaspoon salt
½	cup vegetable shortening
5-6	tablespoons cold water
6	cups vegetable oil

1. Combine flour, salt in bowl; cut in shortening with pastry blender until mixture resembles coarse crumbs; sprinkle water over mixture; work in with fork; form dough into ball.

2. Divide dough into 3 portions; roll each portion out evenly on lightly floured board; cut out three 8-inch circles; cut each circle in half.

3. Place filling in center of each half circle (see following recipes); brush edges of dough with water; fold dough to make quarter circle; pinch edges of dough; crimp with fork.

4. Pour oil into *6-quart Low Pressure Cooker/Fryer*; preheat oil 10-11 minutes to 375°F. (on deep fat thermometer) at setting #9 (high heat); using slotted spoon, place pies into oil, one at a time; brown 3 minutes; clamp on cover.

5. Reduce to setting #7 (medium heat); cook 4 minutes under pressure; turn off; reduce pressure; remove pies with slotted spoon; drain on paper towels.

Makes 6

Fruit-Nut Filling

2	tablespoons butter or margarine
2	tablespoons brown sugar
2	tablespoons honey
½	cup raisins or currants
½	cup chopped nuts
½	teaspoon cinnamon
	Sifted confectioners sugar

1. In *1-quart Sauce Pan,* melt butter; blend in brown sugar, honey; remove from heat; add raisins, nuts, cinnamon; blend thoroughly; cool.

2. Use 2 level tablespoons filling per pie; dust fried pies with sugar.

Savory Filling

¼	pound ground beef
1	clove garlic, minced
¼	cup canned tomato sauce
2	tablespoons raisins
2	tablespoons chopped black olives
1	tablespoon minced onion
¼	teaspoon salt
¼	teaspoon cumin
	Pinch cinnamon
	Pinch cloves

1. Preheat *7-inch Straight-Sided Fry Pan* over medium heat about 2 minutes or until drops of water dance on dry pan surface; sauté ground beef 2 minutes or until lightly browned; drain off drippings.

2. Add remaining ingredients; blend well; reduce heat to low; cook 5-6 minutes, stirring frequently; cool.

3. Use 2½ tablespoons filling per pie.

65

MENU SUGGESTIONS

assorted fruit juices
CRAN-ORANGE COFFEECAKE
eggs benedict
coffee

Mimosas (Champagne and orange juice)
TOAD-IN-THE-HOLE
stuffed baked tomatoes
assorted pastries
fresh fruit and cheese board

Bloody Marys
HAM CREPES
SAVORY FLAKY FRIED PIES
tossed mixed salad
BERRY TRIFLE

STUFFED PORK ROAST
broccoli spears with clarified butter
APPLE-COOKIE CRUMBLE

REUBIN'S CORNED BEEF
sauerkraut with orange sections
spätzle or dumplings
German chocolate cake

BEEF-BARLEY SOUP
tossed salad
coffee and cookies

cream of mushroom soup
BUBBLE-AND-SQUEAK
Harvard beets
spice cake

STIR-FRIED SALAD
whole grain breads
CREPES WITH FRUIT SAUCE

FARMER'S OMELET
Waldorf salad
cheese and crackers

A TOUCH OF CLASS

"A pot luck supper? What a great idea! Have you decided what you'll make?"

"I was thinking that a bouillabaisse might be fun."

"Mmmmm. Sounds hard to make, though."

"Not at all. It's just a fancy name for fish stew."

Steak and potatoes with Mom's apple pie for dessert are considered a traditional item on the American menu. And, since many of us hail from roots that favored the plain and simple in life, recipes with names that are unfamiliar and difficult to pronounce can look forbidding.

First impressions, however, can be deceiving. Cuisine with a continental touch holds many surprises for the palate, and a few more for the inquisitive cook.

For example, the trick to making an entrée that has a touch of the Greek Isles is as near to you as the closest supermarket dairy case: a container of yogurt. The key to cassoulet includes the can of beans already in your kitchen cabinet.

Recipes that sound and look just a little bit fancier than ordinary fare needn't be more complicated to prepare than good old American meatloaf. And the best part of trying fancy recipes is that they are impressive.

The recipes in this chapter were selected for their special combinations of ease of preparation and dramatic result. A few require a spice you may not often use, and some involve familiar ingredients in new and exciting ways. But none of the dishes in this chapter is difficult; most, in fact, are quite easy.

So here's to candelabra, cut crystal and bouillabaisse! ■

67

MEDITERRANEAN KABOBS
Yogurt adds a Middle-Eastern accent to this easy appetizer.

2	pounds boned chicken breasts
2	tablespoons plain yogurt
1½	teaspoons curry powder
1	teaspoon lemon juice
1	teaspoon vinegar
¼	teaspoon salt
⅛	teaspoon dry mustard
⅛	teaspoon dried mint flakes
2	tablespoons chopped chutney
¼	cup plain yogurt

1. Remove skin from chicken; cut chicken into fifty-six 1-inch cubes; add yogurt, curry powder, lemon juice, vinegar, salt, dry mustard, mint; blend well; refrigerate 1 hour.

2. Allowing a 1-inch space from skewer handle, thread 7 chicken cubes on each skewer; attach skewer guards; insert skewers into *Kabob-It* base; place glass cover over food; kabob 16-18 minutes or until done.

3. Combine yogurt, chutney; serve as a dip with chicken.

Makes 56

RUMAKI
Chicken livers wrapped in bacon; makes a tempting appetizer.

10	whole chicken livers (14-oz)
½	cup soy sauce
¼	cup port wine
½	teaspoon ginger
14	slices bacon

1. Quarter chicken livers; combine with soy sauce, wine, ginger; cover; refrigerate at least 1 hour.

2. Cut bacon slices into thirds; wrap piece of bacon around each chicken liver; secure with toothpicks, having toothpicks parallel to cut ends of bacon.

3. Allowing a 1-inch space from skewer handle, thread 5 chicken livers on each skewer; attach skewer guards; insert skewers into *Kabob-It* base; place glass cover over food; kabob 25-28 minutes or until bacon is crisp.

Makes 40

VICHYSSOISE
Adaptation of the famous French soup, made with potatoes.

2	pounds potatoes, peeled, diced
3	cups chopped leeks*
6	cups water
1	teaspoon salt
¼	teaspoon pepper
1	cup milk
½	cup heavy cream
2	tablespoons chopped chives

1. Combine potatoes, leeks, water, salt, pepper in *6-quart Low Pressure Cooker/Fryer;* clamp on cover; bring up pressure on setting #9 (high heat); reduce to setting #2 (low heat); cook 20 minutes; turn off; reduce pressure.

2. Beat mixture with electric mixer until smooth; add milk, cream; refrigerate until serving time; sprinkle with chopped chives. If desired, soup may be served warm.

Makes 2 quarts

*May substitute regular onions.

68

CRABMEAT NEWBERG
Chunks of crabmeat in sherry-scented sauce, in a pastry shell.

4	frozen patty shells
1	tablespoon butter or margarine
2	tablespoons chopped onions
¼	cup sherry
½	cup heavy cream
1	package (16-oz) frozen crabmeat, thawed
3	egg yolks, slightly beaten
	Pinch cayenne pepper

1. Bake patty shells on *15½ x 12-inch Cookie Sheet* following package directions.

2. Melt butter in *2-quart Sauce Pan* over medium heat; add onions; cook until translucent; add sherry, continuing to cook 6-8 minutes or until ½ remains; add cream, crabmeat; simmer 5 minutes.

3. Stir 2 tablespoons hot cream mixture into beaten egg yolks, then return to pan, stirring rapidly; remove from heat; stir in cayenne; spoon into patty shells; garnish with parsley sprigs, as desired.

Makes 4 servings

BOUILLABAISSE
American variation of a classic "fisherman's stew."

2	cups sliced onions
½	cup chopped fresh parsley
2	bay leaves
1	clove garlic, minced
1	can (28-oz) tomatoes, drained
1½	cups white wine
1	cup clam juice
¼	cup water
1	teaspoon basil
1	teaspoon thyme
	Salt, pepper
1	pound swordfish (2″ pieces)
1	pound flounder (2″ pieces)
1	pound scallops

1. Combine onions, parsley, bay leaves, garlic, tomatoes, wine, clam juice, water, basil, thyme in *6-quart Low Pressure Cooker/Fryer;* season with salt, pepper to taste; clamp on cover; bring up pressure on setting #9 (high heat); reduce to setting #2 (low heat); cook 20 minutes; turn off; let stand 5 minutes, then reduce pressure.

2. Stir in swordfish, flounder, scallops; clamp on cover; bring up pressure on setting #9 (high heat); reduce pressure to setting #2 (low heat); cook 5 minutes; turn off; reduce pressure; serve immediately with hot crusty bread, as desired.

Makes 6-8 servings

SOLE IN BUTTER SAUCE
A delicious sauce enhances the light, flaky fish—elegant!

1	large onion, finely chopped
1	small carrot, finely chopped
1½	pounds sole fillets
	Salt, pepper
½	cup white wine
½	cup water
2	tablespoons lemon juice
1	cup butter
¼	cup chopped fresh parsley

1. Spread onions, carrots over bottom of *11½ x 9 x 2-inch Bake & Roast Pan;* arrange fish fillets on top; season with salt, pepper to taste; add wine, water; cover with aluminum foil.

2. Poach in oven 20-25 minutes at 350°F. or until fish flakes; remove fish to serving platter; keep warm; strain juices into *2-quart Sauce Pan;* cook 6-8 minutes over medium heat or until ¼ cup remains; add lemon juice; bring to boil; using wooden spoon or plastic whisk, beat in butter, 1 tablespoon at a time; add parsley; spoon sauce over fish.

Makes 4-6 servings

69

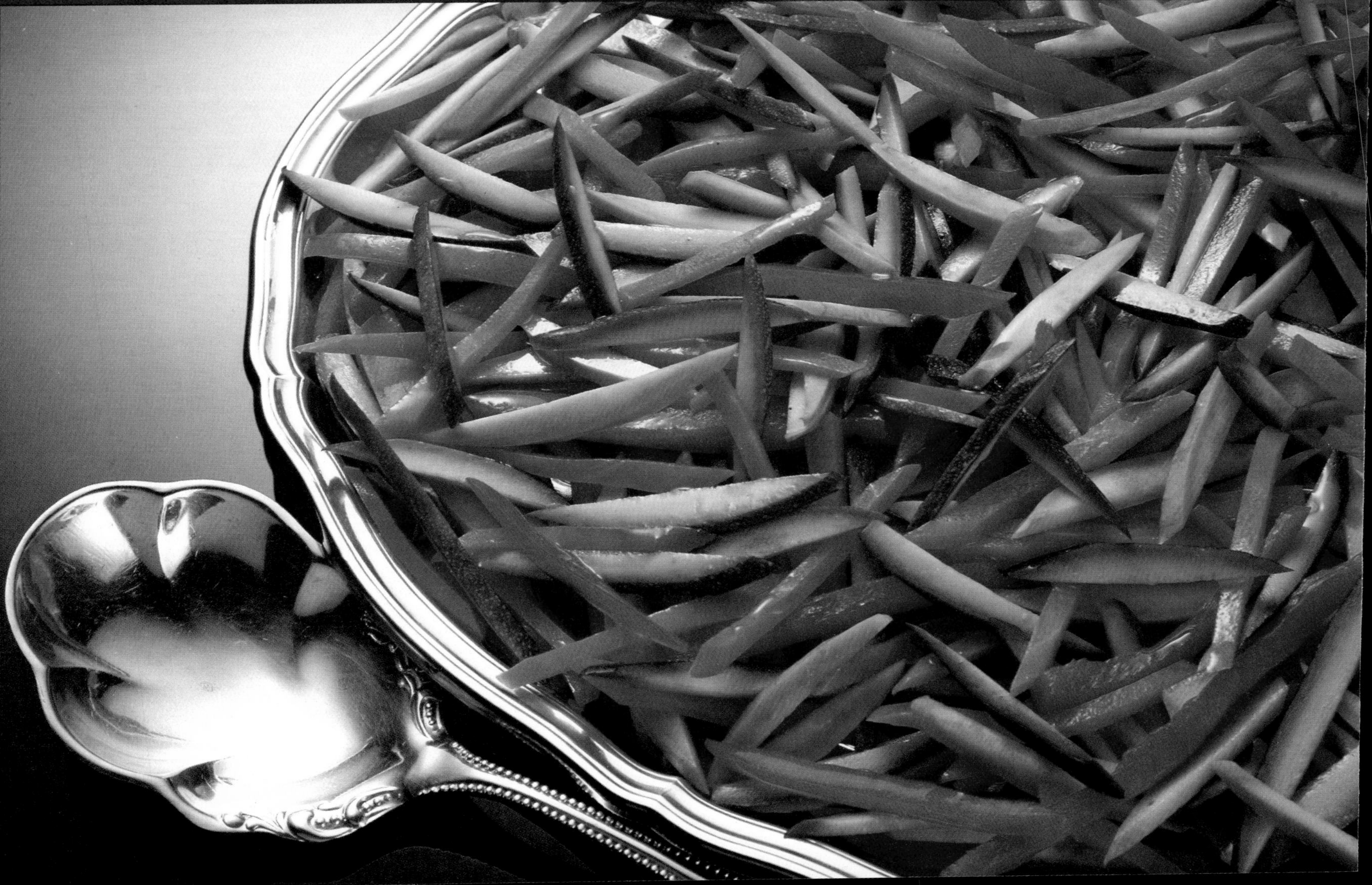

CASSOULET

Quick version of the classic French bean-and-meat casserole.

- 1 pound sweet Italian sausage
- 1 pound hot Italian sausage
- 1 cup chopped onions
- 2 cups sliced carrots
- 1 green pepper, sliced
- 2 chicken legs & thighs, split
- 3 cans (16-oz each) pork & beans
- 1/3 cup white wine
- 1 apple, peeled, grated
- 1 tablespoon Worcestershire sauce
- 1 teaspoon basil
  Sliced green onions

1. Fry sausages in *10-inch Straight-Sided Fry Pan* over medium heat 20-25 minutes or until done; remove; cut into 1-inch pieces; set aside.

2. Sauté onions, carrots, pepper in drippings until lightly browned; remove; set aside; sauté chicken in same pan 10 minutes or until golden brown; remove from heat.

3. Combine beans, wine, apple, Worcestershire sauce, basil, reserved vegetables; pour 1/2 the mixture into *5-quart Dutch Oven;* add sausage, chicken; top with remaining bean mixture; bake 1 hour at 350°F. or until chicken is done; garnish with green onions.

Makes 8 servings

CRISPY MUSHROOM DUCK

Strips of tender duckling sautéed with a mélange of mushrooms.

- 1 duckling (about 5-lb)
- 1/4 cup butter or margarine
- 1 pound fresh mushrooms, sliced
- 1 cup sliced green onions
- 1 clove garlic, minced
- 1 can (15-oz) straw mushrooms, drained
- 1 package (1-oz) dried shiitake mushrooms, soaked
- 6 cups bok choy (2″ pieces)
- 2 tablespoons soy sauce
- 1 tablespoon sesame oil
- 1/4 teaspoon ginger
- 1/4 teaspoon pepper
  Pinch cayenne pepper

1. Place duckling in *11½ x 9 x 2-inch Bake & Roast Pan;* bake 1¼ hours at 400°F. or until skin is crisp; let stand 1 hour; remove meat, skin from bones; shred.

2. Melt butter in *11-inch Chicken Fryer* over medium heat; add fresh mushrooms, onions, garlic; sauté 3 minutes; cut straw mushrooms in half; sliver shiitake mushrooms; add to pan; sauté 3 minutes; add bok choy, soy sauce, oil, ginger, pepper, cayenne; sauté 1 minute; add duck; continue cooking until heated through.

Makes 4 servings

Note: If ingredients are hard to find, may substitute 3½ pound chicken for duckling, 1 pound regular mushrooms for straw and shiitake, 1/4 cup toasted sesame seeds for sesame oil, and spinach for bok choy.

VEGETABLES JARDINIERE

Use any garden-fresh vegetables for this quick-cook technique.

- 2 cups julienne* carrots
- 1/2 cup butter or margarine
- 2 cups julienne red pepper
- 2 cups julienne summer squash
- 2 cups julienne zucchini
- 1 tablespoon lemon juice
  Salt, pepper

1. Pour 1 inch water in *12-inch Chef Style Fry Pan;* bring to boil over medium-high heat; add carrots; reduce heat to medium-low; cook 3 minutes or until carrots are tender-crisp; drain; reserve.

2. Melt butter in pan over medium heat; add red peppers; stir-fry 1 minute; add squash, zucchini; stir-fry 2 minutes; add carrots; stir-fry until heated through; season with lemon juice, salt, pepper to taste; serve at once.

Makes 8 servings

*See page 106 for directions.

Variation:
In winter, may substitute other vegetables; julienne-cut turnips, parsnips, sweet potatoes, etc.

TIP:

Chinese mushrooms, shiitake and straw, are varieties of delicately flavored mushrooms which add an authentic flavor to Oriental dishes. They are available in Chinese markets or specialty food shops.

71

RISOTTO

Famous Italian rice recipe; serve as a first course or side dish.

6	tablespoons olive oil
1	cup chopped onions
1½	cups raw short grain Italian rice
½	cup dry vermouth
2	cloves garlic, minced
½	teaspoon basil
4½	cups (36-oz) canned chicken broth 🍴
2	jars (6-oz each) artichoke hearts, drained
¾	cup grated Parmesan cheese Chopped fresh parsley

1. Heat oil in *5-quart Dutch Oven* over medium heat; sauté onions until translucent; add rice; toss in oil until grains turn white; add vermouth; continue cooking, tossing frequently, until most of liquid is gone.

2. Add garlic, basil, 1½ cups broth; cover; continue to cook; stir occasionally; as liquid is absorbed, add more broth (1½ cups at a time) until all liquid is absorbed, rice is tender but not mushy (takes 30-40 minutes).

3. Add artichoke hearts, Parmesan; toss; sprinkle parsley over top.

Makes 6 servings

SPAGHETTI FLIP

Use any combination of vegetables and cheese for this pasta "pie."

½	pound uncooked spaghetti*
¼	cup chopped onions
1	clove garlic, minced
1	teaspoon dried dill weed
½	teaspoon chervil
⅛	teaspoon pepper
½	cup heavy cream
1	package (10-oz) frozen chopped spinach, thawed
½	cup finely crumbled feta cheese
8	ounces shredded Edam cheese

1. Cook spaghetti in *3-quart Sauce Pan* following package directions; drain; combine with onions, garlic, dill, chervil, pepper, cream; toss thoroughly.

2. Place ½ spaghetti mixture in ungreased *10-inch Chef Style Fry Pan;* squeeze spinach to remove excess moisture; arrange on top; sprinkle with feta, ½ the Edam; top with remaining spaghetti, then remaining Edam.

3. Cover; cook over medium-low heat 25-30 minutes or until bottom is crusty golden brown; invert onto serving plate.

Makes 6 servings

*May substitute 4 cups leftover cooked spaghetti.

PASTA AMATRICIANA

Spicy tomato sauce with bacon, from Southern Italy.

½	pound uncooked rigatoni*
6	large ripe tomatoes
¼	pound bacon (¼" strips)
¼	teaspoon crushed red pepper
½	teaspoon basil
½	teaspoon salt
½	teaspoon sugar
¼	teaspoon pepper
¼	cup grated Parmesan cheese

1. Cook rigatoni in *3-quart Sauce Pan* following package directions; drain; peel, seed and coarsely chop tomatoes.

2. Cook bacon in *10-inch Straight-Sided Fry Pan* over medium heat until lightly browned; pour off all but 2 tablespoons fat; add tomatoes, red pepper, basil, salt, sugar, pepper; bring to boil; cover; reduce heat to low; simmer 10 minutes.

3. Remove cover; continue simmering another 10 minutes; serve over rigatoni; sprinkle with Parmesan.

Makes 4 servings

*May substitute elbow macaroni or other pasta products.

TIP:

Don't throw out that leftover spaghetti or other varieties of pasta! Just toss in a bit of oil, wrap tightly in plastic wrap or store in air-tight container and refrigerate. When ready to use, bring a large pot of water to a boil. Drop in spaghetti for 1-2 minutes, just enough to reheat, then drain.

KIELBASA EN CROUTE
*Crusty variation on a sausage favorite—
great cold lunch.*

1   pound kielbasa
**1   package (17 ¼-oz) frozen puff
        pastry sheets**
1   egg yolk
3   tablespoons milk
1   teaspoon Dijon mustard
1   cup mayonnaise
        Dijon mustard

1. Cut kielbasa into 2 equal lengths; thaw
   pastry; roll out each sheet to be 1 inch
   longer than each kielbasa piece; place
   kielbasa on pastry; roll up; pinch seams;
   place on *15½ x 12-inch Cookie Sheet.*

2. Combine egg yolk, milk, mustard; brush
   over top of rolls; bake 20-25 minutes at
   425°F. or until golden brown; cool
   slightly before slicing.

3. Combine mayonnaise, mustard to taste;
   serve with kielbasa slices.

Makes 6 servings

POPPYCOCK
A very sophisticated popcorn snack.

½   cup popcorn kernels
1   package (14-oz) caramels
¼   cup milk
2   cups pecans*

1. Make popcorn in *Popcorn Pumper;*
   measure 2 quarts; store remaining for
   later use.

2. Combine caramels, milk in *5-quart
   Dutch Oven;* heat over low heat until
   caramels melt, mixture is smooth; stir
   frequently; remove from heat.

3. Add popcorn, pecans; toss together;
   pour onto *15½ x 12-inch Cookie Sheet*
   to harden; break into clusters.

Makes 10 cups

*May substitute almonds, walnuts,
hazelnuts or Brazil nuts.

73

CROUSTADE

Traditional apple dessert of Gascony; flaky and luscious.

2 **pounds apples, peeled, cored**
½ **cup sugar**
¼ **cup apple brandy**
2 **teaspoons grated orange peel**
¼ **teaspoon vanilla**
½ **pound packaged phyllo dough**
⅓ **cup butter or margarine, melted**
8 **prunes,* cooked**
 Confectioners sugar

1. Thinly slice apples; place in *3-quart Sauce Pan* along with sugar; cook over low heat 20-25 minutes or until apples are soft; add brandy, orange peel, vanilla; cool.

2. Fold each sheet of dough in half, lengthwise; arrange in spoke-like pattern on *15½ x 12-inch Cookie Sheet;* brush each sheet with butter; arrange apple mixture in center of dough; place prunes around apples; bring dough up over apples to meet in center; twist ends.

3. Place on low rack of oven; bake 15 minutes at 400°F., then 20 minutes at 350°F. or until golden brown; serve warm sprinkled with confectioners sugar.

Makes 8-10 servings

*Uncooked prunes may be soaked in apple brandy from 2 days to 2 months; cooked as needed for more flavorful results; store in refrigerator.

PARTY RYE LOAVES

Delicious homemade rye bread, a perfect base for canapés.

2 **cups rye flour**
1 **cup all purpose flour**
2 **tablespoons sugar**
2 **teaspoons salt**
2 **packages active dry yeast**
1¼ **cups water**
½ **cup milk**
2 **tablespoons butter or margarine**
1 **tablespoon molasses**
2½ **cups all purpose flour**
1 **egg white**
1 **tablespoon water**
1 **tablespoon caraway or sesame seeds**

1. In large bowl, thoroughly mix rye flour, white flour, sugar, salt, yeast.

2. Combine water, milk, butter, molasses in *1-quart Sauce Pan;* heat over low heat until very warm (120°-130°F.); gradually add to dry ingredients using low speed of electric mixer; beat 2 minutes on medium speed; add 1 cup white flour; beat 2 minutes on high speed, scraping bowl occasionally; with spoon stir in additional white flour to make soft dough.

3. Turn dough out onto lightly floured board; knead 8-10 minutes or until smooth, elastic; shape dough into ball; let rest 20 minutes.

4. Divide dough into 4 equal pieces; shape each piece into a 14-inch long loaf; place loaves on 2 ungreased *15½ x 12-inch Cookie Sheets,* 2 loaves per sheet; cover with towel; let rise 1 hour or until doubled in bulk.

5. Make diagonal slashes on top of loaves; beat egg white with water until frothy; brush on loaves; sprinkle with seeds; bake 25 minutes at 375°F. or until golden brown; cool on wire racks.

Makes 4 loaves

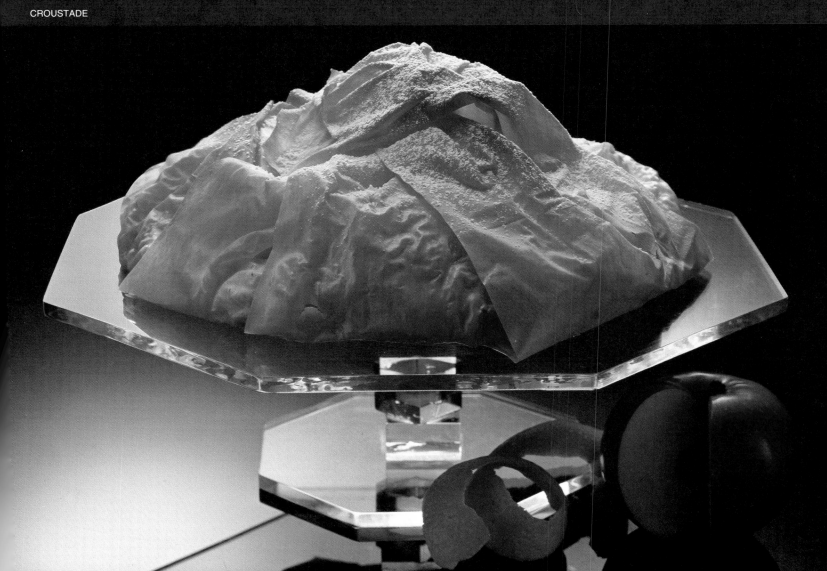

MENU SUGGESTIONS

wonton soup
CRISPY MUSHROOM DUCK
rice
California Chablis
almond cookies
tea

BOUILLABAISSE
garlic bread
tossed green salad
very dry white wine, such as Muscadet
CROUSTADE

VICHYSSOISE
SOLE IN BUTTER SAUCE
VEGETABLES JARDINIERE
white Burgundy
lime sherbet with ginger snaps

RUMAKI
PASTA AMATRICIANA
arugula and endive salad
Valpolicella
fresh fruit and cheese board

CASSOULET
tossed green salad
California Barbera
fresh orange slices with Kirsch

PARTY RYE LOAVES ~ Brie
CRABMEAT NEWBURG
peas with mushrooms
Alsace Riesling
chocolate mousse

MEDITERRANEAN KABOBS
lamb chops
duchess potatoes
watercress salad
Greek Demestica
rum raisin ice cream

RISOTTO
roast chicken with rosemary
zucchini with red pepper
dry white or rosé wine
frozen raspberry yogurt

KIELBASA EN CROUTE
German potato salad
pickled onions and cucumbers
beer, German or Austrian white wine
assorted cheeses

ROMANTIC NOTIONS

"What are you doing on your anniversary?"

"Oh, this year we plan to stay home."

"Getting too old for romance, eh?"

"Not really. We're going to prepare the same meal that we ate in the little French restaurant where we had our first date."

Few married couples will deny that "wining and dining" together played an important role in their courtship. Many an engagement ring has been exchanged over a candlelit dinner, and probably most women and men will remember, perhaps with a chuckle, the first meal they ever cooked for that special person in their lives.

Love and appetite have always been related, although the connection varies with the individual. Cupid's arrow causes some people to skip meals, while it makes others ravenous. Scientific studies have now revealed that the same chemical naturally produced by the body of someone "in love"—phenylethylamine—is provided in big doses by chocolate, which may explain an oft-reported craving by the lovelorn for this sweet food.

Whatever science or psychology may contribute to our knowledge of the relationship between food and romance, nearly everyone will agree that a blossoming—or mature—relationship calls for some special, intimate meal plans.

The recipes in this chapter have all been created to serve romantically inclined couples. They are designed to be just a bit extraordinary in taste and appearance to match that most extraordinary of human phenomena— being in love. ■

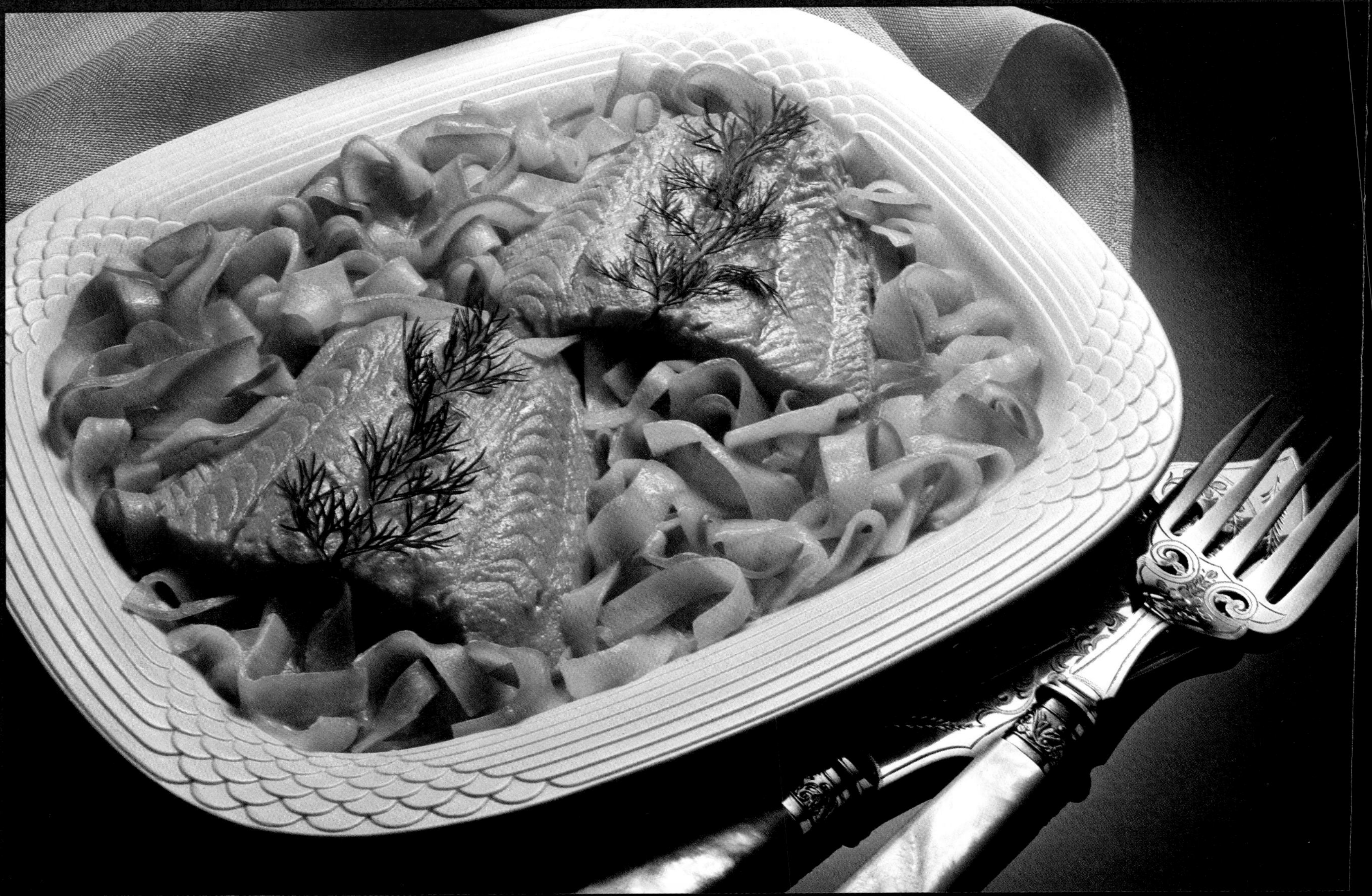

POACHED SALMON
Beautiful color, light texture, easy on the waistline.

- 1   **quart water**
- 2   **tablespoons vinegar**
- 1   **teaspoon salt**
- 2   **salmon fillets (½-lb each)**
       Fresh dill sprigs

1. Combine water, vinegar, salt in *10-inch Straight-Sided Fry Pan;* bring to boil over medium-high heat; reduce heat to low; add salmon; cover; poach 6-8 minutes or until fish flakes.

2. Garnish with fresh dill sprigs or dill butter rosettes, as desired.

Makes 2 servings

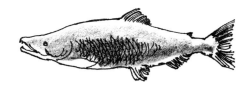

SAVORY STUFFED ARTICHOKES
Bread crumbs add texture and spices add flavor.

- 2   **large artichokes**
- 2   **cups water**
- 2   **tablespoons olive oil**
- 1   **cup chopped onions**
- 1   **large clove garlic, minced**
- 3   **cups fresh bread crumbs**
- ¼   **cup grated Parmesan cheese**
- 2   **tablespoons chopped fresh parsley**
- 1   **teaspoon anchovy paste (optional)**
- ¼   **teaspoon basil**
- ¼   **teaspoon oregano**
       Pinch crushed red pepper
- 2   **tablespoons butter or margarine, melted**

1. Wash artichokes; cut off thorny tips of leaves with kitchen shears; place in *6-quart Low Pressure Cooker/Fryer* with water; clamp on cover; bring up pressure on setting #9 (high heat); reduce to setting #2 (low heat); cook 16 minutes; turn off; reduce pressure.

2. Heat oil in *10-inch Chef Style Fry Pan* over medium heat; sauté onions until translucent; add remaining ingredients; cook 3-4 minutes, stirring constantly; spoon stuffing between leaves of artichokes; return to pan; drizzle with butter, bake 10 minutes at 350°F.

Makes 2 servings

OYSTER STEW
Simple and elegant first course.

- 1   **cup heavy cream**
- 1   **cup diced, cooked potatoes**
- 1   **pint oysters with liquid**
- 2   **tablespoons butter or margarine**
       Salt, pepper
       Paprika
       Chopped fresh parsley

1. Heat cream in *2-quart Sauce Pan* over medium heat until it just starts to simmer; add potatoes, oysters with liquid; cook over low heat 3-6 minutes or until oysters float to top.

2. Add butter; season with salt, pepper to taste; continue simmering until butter melts; remove from heat; sprinkle with paprika, parsley; serve at once.

Makes 2¾ cups

79

COLD MARINATED SWORDFISH

An impressive-looking dish; the onions become sweet when cooked.

2 tablespoons olive oil
1 large onion, cut in rings
2 tablespoons butter or margarine
10 ounces swordfish, cubed
1 bay leaf
¼ cup red wine vinegar
½ teaspoon salt
¼ teaspoon white pepper
Pinch coriander
Chopped fresh parsley
Salt, white pepper

1. Heat oil in *12-inch Chef Style Fry Pan* over medium heat; sauté onions until limp; remove from pan; reserve.

2. Melt butter in pan; sauté swordfish 3-5 minutes or until just firm to the touch; remove from heat; add onions, bay leaf, vinegar, salt, pepper, coriander; pour into shallow bowl; cover; refrigerate at least 3 hours.

3. Remove bay leaf; let stand at room temperature 10-15 minutes before serving; sprinkle with parsley; season with salt, pepper to taste; serve on lettuce leaves, as desired.

Makes 2 servings

CHICKEN IN CHAMPAGNE

The most romantic wine creates a most romantic dish.

1 large chicken breast, boned
⅔ cup champagne
1 tablespoon finely chopped onions
1 small clove garlic, minced
¼ teaspoon salt
Pinch white pepper
6 tablespoons unsalted butter
2 tablespoons chopped fresh parsley

1. Remove skin from breast; split in half; place between several thicknesses of waxed paper; pound until thin; place in *8-inch Round Cake Pan*; add champagne, onions, garlic, salt, pepper; cover with sheet of waxed paper; poach in oven 25 minutes at 350°F. or until tender; remove chicken to serving platter; keep warm.

2. Pour juices into *7-inch Straight-Sided Fry Pan*; bring to boil over medium heat; continue to cook until ¼ cup remains; beat in butter with wooden spoon (1 tablespoon at a time) until smooth; stir in parsley; spoon sauce over chicken.

Makes 2 servings

VEAL CHOPS FONTINA

The cheese stuffing melts for a gooey surprise.

2 thick veal chops (¾-lb each)
2 ounces fontina cheese, thinly sliced
¼ cup flour
¼ teaspoon salt
Pinch white pepper
1 egg, slightly beaten
2 cups fresh bread crumbs
¼ cup clarified butter*
Salt, white pepper
Chopped fresh parsley

1. Make pocket in both chops, cutting to bone; pound meat gently until ½-inch thick; place cheese slices in pockets; secure with toothpicks.

2. Combine flour, salt, pepper; coat chops with flour mixture; dip into egg; coat with crumbs; refrigerate 30 minutes.

3. Melt butter in *12-inch Chef Style Fry Pan* over medium heat; sauté chops 6-7 minutes on both sides or until tender, golden brown; season with salt, pepper to taste; sprinkle with chopped parsley.

Makes 2 servings

*See page 108 for directions.

MARTINI LAMB CHOPS

Make three martinis: two for drinking and one for the chops!

1   **teaspoon olive oil**
4   **loin lamb chops (¾" thick)**
    Salt
6   **tablespoons gin**
2   **tablespoons dry vermouth**
    Pinch thyme
    Chopped fresh parsley

1. Heat oil in *10-inch Chef Style Fry Pan* over medium heat; sauté lamb chops 4-5 minutes; turn; sprinkle with salt; sauté 4-5 minutes or until desired doneness; remove from pan.

2. Pour off any accumulated fat; add gin, vermouth, thyme; simmer until 3 tablespoons remain; add parsley; serve sauce with chops.

Makes 2 servings

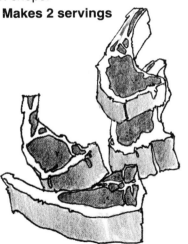

GASPAR'S BITOQUES

The most elegant hamburger you (and yours) will ever eat!

½   **pound ground beef tenderloin**
¾   **cup fresh bread crumbs**
2   **tablespoons heavy cream**
3   **tablespoons butter, softened**
½   **teaspoon salt**
    Pinch white pepper
2   **tablespoons flour**
1   **egg, beaten**
¾   **cup fresh bread crumbs**
2   **tablespoons butter or margarine**

1. Combine beef, crumbs, cream, butter, salt, pepper; mix thoroughly; shape into 2 patties; refrigerate 30 minutes.

2. Coat patties with flour; dip into egg; finally coat with crumbs; refrigerate 30 minutes.

3. Melt butter in *10-inch Chef Style Fry Pan* over medium heat; sauté patties 8 minutes on each side or until golden brown, cooked to desired doneness.

Makes 2 servings

STIR-FRIED CUCUMBERS

Thin strips are quick-cooked for a delicate, translucent result.

1   **large cucumber**
1   **tablespoon butter or margarine**
    Salt, pepper
    Dill sprigs

1. Peel cucumber; slice in half lengthwise; scoop out seeds and discard; cut cucumber halves into 2-inch pieces; cut each piece into very thin strips.

2. Melt butter in *8-inch Chef Style Fry Pan* over medium heat; add cucumber strips; stir-fry 2 minutes or until just tender; season with salt, pepper to taste; garnish with dill sprigs.

Makes 2 servings

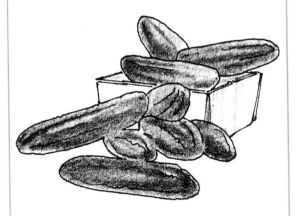

EASY ASPARAGUS

No need for a special cooker for this delightful dish.

12	asparagus spears (½-lb)
1	cup water
¼	teaspoon salt
⅔	cup hollandaise sauce♟

1. Snap bottom ends off asparagus spears; peel up to buds.
2. Bring water, salt to boil in *10-inch Chef Style Fry Pan* over medium-high heat; add asparagus; cover; cook 6-10 minutes for tender-crisp; 10-14 minutes for tender; drain; serve with hollandaise sauce.*

Makes 2 servings

*May substitute melted butter seasoned with lemon juice to taste.

PRALINE CHOCOLATE MOUSSE

A sophisticated mousse with the subtle taste of hazelnuts.

2	ounces unsweetened chocolate
2	tablespoons butter or margarine
2	eggs, separated
⅔	cup praline powder♟
	Pinch salt
½	cup heavy cream, whipped
2	meringue shells♟

1. Melt chocolate, butter in *1-quart Sauce Pan* over medium-low heat; cool slightly.
2. Beat together egg yolks, praline powder 3-4 minutes or until slightly thickened; add chocolate mixture; blend thoroughly.
3. Add salt to egg whites; beat until peaks form; stir ⅓ into chocolate mixture; fold in remaining egg whites; fold in whipped cream; refrigerate at least 1 hour; spoon into meringue shells; garnish with chocolate leaves or curls, as desired.

Makes 2 servings

CHESTNUT PUREE

An unusual side dish; pairs beautifully with poultry or ham.

½	pound chestnuts, cooked, peeled
1	small celery stalk, finely chopped
¼	cup heavy cream
2	tablespoons butter or margarine
	Madeira
	Salt, pepper

1. Combine chestnuts, celery, cream, butter in *2-quart Sauce Pan;* cover; bring to a simmer over medium heat; reduce heat to low; simmer 5 minutes.
2. Spoon mixture into blender container; blend on low speed until smooth; season with Madeira, salt, pepper to taste; serve as a vegetable.

Makes 2 servings

82

CHOCOLATE RUM TRUFFLES
Delicious denouement for a romantic meal.

8	ounces semi-sweet chocolate
½	cup butter or margarine
3	egg yolks
3	tablespoons dark rum
½	cup unsweetened cocoa powder

1. Melt chocolate, butter in *2-quart Sauce Pan* over medium-low heat; add egg yolks, rum; beat with wooden spoon or plastic whisk until well-blended; pour into bowl; refrigerate 1 hour or until firm enough to handle.
2. Shape mixture into thirty-six 1-inch balls (about 1 teaspoon each); roll in cocoa; refrigerate several hours or until serving time.

Makes 3 dozen

CHILLED CHERRY SOUP
Swedish in origin, a sweet beginning, or end, to any meal.

1	can (1-lb) pitted dark sweet cherries, drained
2	cups water
2	tablespoons sugar
1	tablespoon lemon juice
⅛	teaspoon cinnamon
2	teaspoons cornstarch
½	cup white wine
2	tablespoons whipped cream

1. Combine cherries, water, sugar, lemon juice, cinnamon in *2-quart Sauce Pan;* bring to a simmer over medium heat; combine cornstarch, wine; add to cherry mixture, stirring until smooth; boil 2 minutes or until slightly thickened.
2. Ladle mixture into blender container; blend on low speed until smooth; chill; garnish with whipped cream.

Makes 3 cups

TIP:

In order to whip cream successfully you will need to use no less than ¼ cup heavy cream. The cream will double in volume when whipped. Use the 2 tablespoons required in this recipe; then save the rest for after-dinner coffee. Whipped cream can be stored in the refrigerator for 24 hours.

RASPBERRY TARTLETS
Use frozen shells for a quick, easy and elegant dessert.

2	frozen patty shells
¼	cup raspberry preserves
¼	cup heavy cream, whipped
½	cup fresh raspberries

1. Bake patty shells in *8-inch Round Cake Pan* following package directions.
2. Melt preserves in *1-quart Sauce Pan* over low heat; spoon into patty shells; top with ½ the whipped cream, all the raspberries; garnish with remaining whipped cream.

Makes 2 servings

Variations:
May substitute blueberries, sliced strawberries, blackberries with appropriate preserves.

84

MENU SUGGESTIONS

POACHED SALMON
STIR-FRIED CUCUMBERS
new potatoes
fine white Burgundy or California Riesling
lemon mousse

VEAL CHOPS FONTINA
marinated artichoke hearts
buttered noodles
light red Burgundy, such as Beaujolais
strawberries in cream

CHICKEN IN CHAMPAGNE
EASY ASPARAGUS
parsley rice
Champagne or dry white wine
CHOCOLATE RUM TRUFFLES

GASPAR'S BITOQUES
ratatouille
scalloped potatoes
California Zinfandel
raspberry sherbet with cookies

MARTINI LAMB CHOPS
broiled tomatoes
peas with mint
French bread
California Cabernet Sauvignon
fruit and cheese

beef consommé with croutons
COLD MARINATED SWORDFISH
melon balls
French rolls
white Burgundy
CREME BRULEE

MENU SUGGESTIONS

scallops in white wine
watercress salad
rolls
California Riesling
PRALINE CHOCOLATE MOUSSE

CHILLED CHERRY SOUP
broiled lemon chicken
EASY ASPARAGUS
wild rice
dry white Burgundy
buttered almond ice cream

OYSTER STEW
oyster crackers
veal scallopini
tossed green salad
Champagne or dry white wine
orange sherbet

SAVORY STUFFED ARTICHOKES
filet mignon
sautéed mushrooms
red Bordeaux
peaches in cream

stuffed pork chops
CHESTNUT PUREE
julienne carrots and zucchini
young red Burgundy
applesauce with yogurt

boiled lobster
clarified butter
tossed green salad
non-vintage Champagne or French Chablis
RASPBERRY TARTLETS

A MOVEABLE FEAST

"What's on the tube tonight?"

"A Bogart movie!"

"But it starts at 7:00. I'll never finish making dinner in time."

"How about kabobs? We'll skewer our dinner and cook it in the family room."

There are lots of good reasons to stay out of the kitchen. A special TV movie, some old friends who dropped by, or just a personal need to get away from the range can be the inspiration for changing the location for meal preparation. And with the wide variety of small electric appliances available today, portable cooking can be an option for anyone.

You can even bring a backyard barbecue indoors. Simply prepare fresh

foods for cooking in the kitchen, load them into a basket or onto a tray, and move your meal where the action is. Once you try it, chances are you'll find plenty of reasons to repeat the experience.

The recipes in this chapter were designed for use with several different kinds of small electric cooking appliances. They range from spur-of-the-moment snacks to party fare—a variety of ideas for almost any occasion.

Next time you're in the mood to cook someplace other than in the kitchen, take that small appliance out of the cabinet and make yourself a moveable feast! ■

SMOKEY POPCORN

Popcorn snack that's an out-of-hand appetizer; great with TV!

½   **cup popcorn kernels**
¼   **cup butter or margarine, melted**
½   **pound sliced bacon, cooked**
½   **cup thinly sliced green onions**

1. Prepare popcorn in *Popcorn Pumper*; measure 2 quarts; store remaining for later use.
2. Cool butter slightly; drizzle over popcorn; crumble bacon; add with green onions; toss together.

Makes 1½ quarts

TIP:

Cool butter slightly before pouring over hot popcorn. This will reduce the shrinkage of the popped kernels.

HERB CURRY

Have your guests "shoot" their own canapés on a variety of crackers.

1   **package (8-oz) cream cheese**
2   **tablespoons sour cream**
1½ **teaspoons lemon juice**
1   **teaspoon grated lemon peel**
1   **teaspoon chopped parsley**
½   **teaspoon Worcestershire sauce**
½   **teaspoon seasoned salt**
¼   **teaspoon curry powder**
¼   **teaspoon salt**
     Assorted crackers, vegetables

1. Combine cheese, sour cream, lemon juice, lemon peel, parsley and seasonings; beat thoroughly until smooth.
2. Fill barrel of *Super Shooter* with curry mixture; pipe mixture onto desired crackers or vegetables using decorator tip.

Makes 1⅓ cups

SAVORY CROUTONS

Tasty, crunchy bread cubes for snacking or toppings.

1   **loaf French/Italian bread, unsliced**
½   **cup butter or margarine, melted**
½   **teaspoon curry powder**
½   **teaspoon onion powder**
½   **teaspoon garlic salt**

1. Cut forty-eight ¾-inch cubes from bread; allowing a 1-inch space from skewer handle, thread 6 bread cubes on each skewer, piercing through crust first; attach skewer guards.
2. In small bowl, combine butter, curry powder, onion powder, garlic salt; blend thoroughly; brush on all sides of bread cubes.
3. Insert skewers into *Kabob-It* base; place glass cover over food; kabob 8-9 minutes or until nicely browned.

Makes 48

PERRITOS

These cut-up franks make a tasty hot appetizer—Tex-Mex style.

8   hot dogs
½   cup mild taco sauce
1   tablespoon cumin
¾   cup crushed tortilla chips

1. Cut each hot dog crosswise into 4 pieces; allowing a 1-inch space from skewer handle, thread 4 pieces lengthwise on each skewer, leaving ¼-inch space between each; attach skewer guards.

2. Combine taco sauce, cumin; brush mixture on hot dogs; sprinkle with tortilla chips.

3. Insert skewers into *Kabob-It* base; place glass cover over food; kabob 10-12 minutes or until lightly browned, hot inside.

Makes 32

CHICKEN NUGGETS

Skewered chicken, Indonesian-style.

½   cup peanut butter
¼   cup minced onions
¼   cup minced parsley
¼   cup lemon juice
1   tablespoon soy sauce
2   cloves garlic, minced
1   teaspoon coriander
2   pounds boned chicken breasts

1. Combine peanut butter, onions, parsley, lemon juice, soy sauce, garlic, coriander in blender container; blend on low speed until smooth.

2. Remove skin from chicken; cut chicken into fifty-six 1-inch cubes; allowing a 1-inch space from skewer handle, thread 7 chicken cubes on each skewer; attach skewer guards; brush chicken with peanut sauce; refrigerate 30 minutes.

3. Insert skewers into *Kabob-It* base; place glass cover over food; kabob 18-20 minutes or until done.

Makes 56

PORK KABOBS

Sweet and sour sauce adds the Polynesian touch.

1½   pounds boneless lean pork
½   cup apricot preserves
2   tablespoons vinegar
1   tablespoon light brown sugar
¼   teaspoon cloves

1. Cut pork into forty-eight ¾-inch cubes; allowing a 1-inch space from skewer handle, thread 6 pork cubes on each skewer; attach skewer guards; combine preserves, vinegar, brown sugar, cloves; brush on pork.

2. Insert skewers into *Kabob-It* base; place glass cover over food; kabob 21-23 minutes or until done; serve with remaining sauce as dip.

Makes 48

90

TERIYAKI CHICKEN POCKETS

Japanese-style chicken in pita bread makes a unique sandwich.

1½	pounds boned chicken breasts
1	clove garlic, minced
2	tablespoons soy sauce
1	tablespoon ginger
1	tablespoon sherry
6	large-size pita bread, heated
1	cup shredded lettuce
½	cup chopped orange pieces

1. Remove skin from chicken; cut chicken into forty ½-inch strips; combine garlic, soy sauce, ginger, sherry; pour over chicken; cover; refrigerate 1 hour; drain.

2. Allowing a 1-inch space from skewer handle, thread 5 chicken strips on each skewer; attach skewer guards.

3. Insert skewers into *Kabob-It* base; place glass cover over food; kabob 17-18 minutes or until done.

4. Fill pita bread pockets with 1⅓ skewers of chicken, shredded lettuce, orange pieces.

Makes 6 servings

SAUSAGE AND PEPPERS

Make an Italian hero in your own living room.

6	links Italian sausage (¾-lb)
2	medium onions
2	medium red or green peppers
6	hero rolls
½	cup spaghetti sauce
	Salt, pepper

1. Cut each sausage link crosswise into 4 equal pieces; cut onions, red peppers into 24 pieces each; allowing a 1-inch space from skewer handle, alternately thread 3 sausage, 3 onion, 3 red pepper pieces on each skewer; attach skewer guards.

2. Insert skewers into *Kabob-It* base; place glass cover over food; kabob 25-27 minutes or until sausage is done.

3. Spoon spaghetti sauce onto each roll; place 1⅓ skewers of food into each roll; season with salt, pepper to taste.

Makes 6 servings

STUFFED AVOCADO

A beautiful, colorful first course.

1	package (6-oz) frozen crabmeat*, thawed
8	ounces shredded Monterey Jack cheese
½	cup mayonnaise
2	tablespoons chopped pimiento
2	tablespoons lime juice
½	teaspoon Worcestershire sauce
3	drops Tabasco sauce
4	ripe avocados

1. Combine crabmeat, cheese, mayonnaise, pimiento, lime juice, Worcestershire, Tabasco in bowl; beat with electric mixer until smooth.

2. Cut avocados in half, lengthwise; remove pits; fill barrel of *Super Shooter* with crabmeat mixture; pipe mixture into each avocado half using decorator tip.

Makes 8 servings

*May substitute canned crabmeat.

91

92

SURF AND TURF
Economical version of the filet and lobster classic.

¾	**pound flank steak**
1	**large green pepper**
24	**medium-size shrimp, cleaned**
1	**clove garlic, minced**
⅓	**cup chopped onions**
⅓	**cup vegetable oil**
¼	**cup sesame seeds**
3	**tablespoons corn syrup**
2	**tablespoons soy sauce**
¼	**teaspoon ginger**

1. Cut flank steak into twenty-four 3 x ¼-inch strips; cut green pepper into twenty-four 1-inch pieces; place steak, pepper, shrimp in bowl.

2. Combine garlic, onions, oil, sesame seeds, corn syrup, soy sauce, ginger; blend thoroughly; pour over ingredients in bowl; cover; marinate in refrigerator 4 hours or overnight; drain.

3. Allowing a 1-inch space from skewer handle, alternately thread 3 steak strips curved in "C" shape around 3 shrimp with 3 pepper pieces on each skewer; attach skewer guards.

4. Insert skewers into *Kabob-It* base; place glass cover over food; kabob 15-17 minutes or until done; serve on bed of rice, garnished with scallion brushes, as desired.

Makes 4 servings

CRUNCHY POTATO SKINS
A crunchy, appetizing alternative to the potato chip.

4	**large baking potatoes (10-oz each)**
¼	**cup vegetable oil**
	Salt, pepper
8	**ounces sour cream**
¼	**cup fresh snipped chives**

1. Prick potatoes; bake 1½ hours at 350°F. or until done. (Skins should be tender, not dry.)

2. Cut off tip ends of potatoes, then cut each potato crosswise into 4 equal pieces; cut out potato to within ⅛-inch of skin; cut each skin in one place to make 16 long strips. (Reserve potato for later use.)

3. Brush both sides of skins with oil; sprinkle with salt, pepper to taste; allowing a 1-inch space from skewer handle, carefully thread 2 strips on each skewer; attach skewer guards.

4. Insert skewers into *Kabob-It* base; place glass cover over food; kabob 10-11 minutes or until crisp, brown.

5. Combine sour cream, chives; dip potato skins carefully into this mixture.

Makes 16

BANANA LOGS
You can watch them cook while you eat the main course!

½	**cup butter or margarine**
¼	**cup honey or brown sugar**
1	**cup ginger snap crumbs**
1½	**tablespoons grated orange peel**
½	**teaspoon cinnamon**
6	**medium bananas, green tipped**
1	**large apple, unpeeled**

1. Combine butter, honey in *1-quart Sauce Pan*; heat over low heat until butter melts; beat until blended; combine crumbs, orange peel, cinnamon in bowl.

2. Peel bananas; cut crosswise into twenty-four 1½-inch pieces; roll each piece in butter mixture to coat evenly; roll in crumbs.

3. Cut apple into 24 even pieces; allowing a 1-inch space from skewer handle, alternately thread 3 apple pieces and 3 banana logs on each skewer; attach skewer guards.

4. Insert skewers into *Kabob-It* base; place glass cover over food; kabob 7-8 minutes or until just lightly browned.

Makes 24

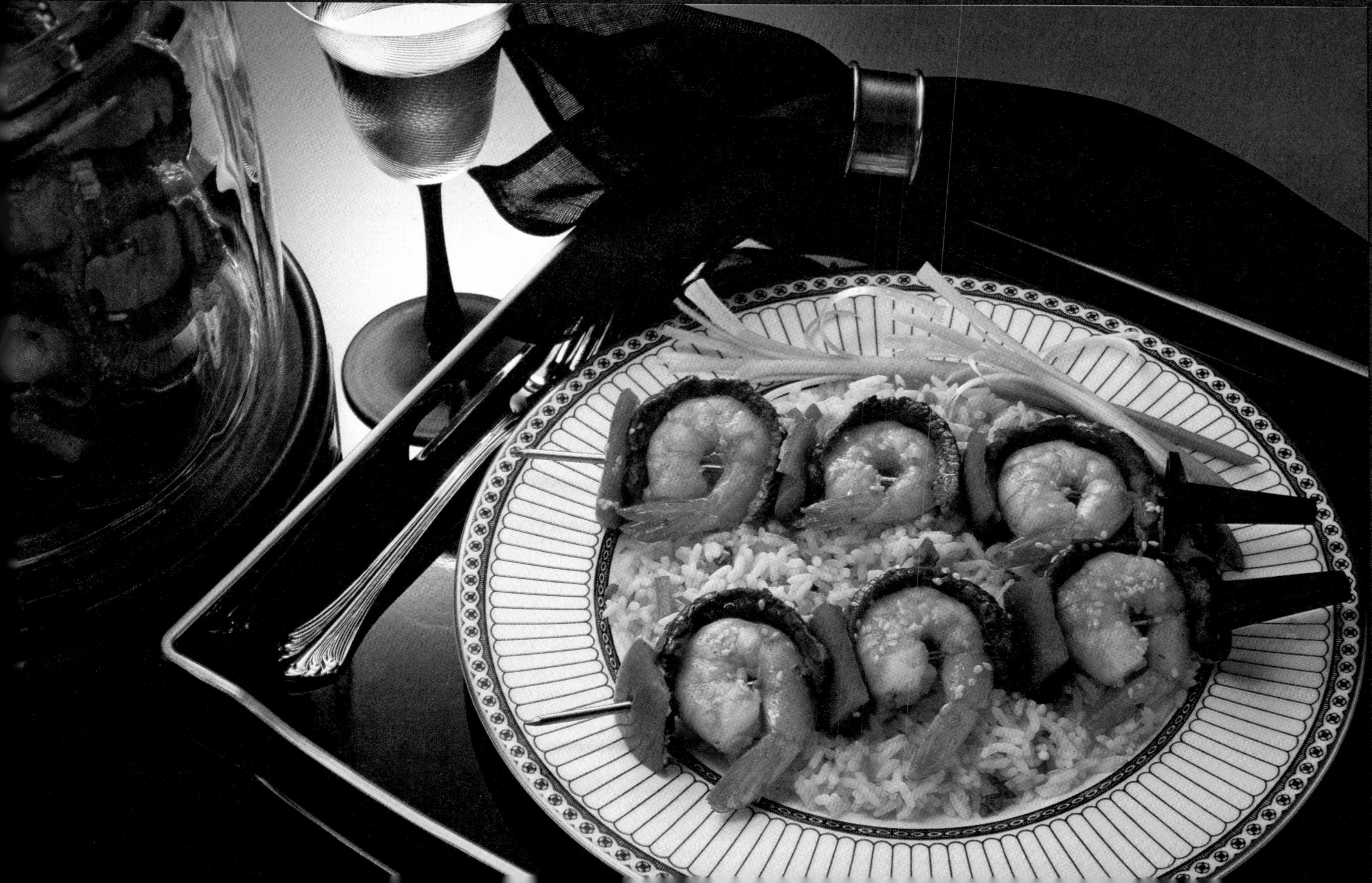

GORP SNACK
Combine kids' favorite ingredients —
a great party treat.

½ cup popcorn kernels
½ cup chopped candy-coated
  chocolate candies
½ cup chopped peanuts
½ cup chopped raisins
2 tablespoons butter or margarine
2 tablespoons honey

1. Prepare popcorn in *Popcorn Pumper*;
   measure 2 quarts; store remaining for
   later use.

2. Add candies, peanuts, raisins; toss
   together; combine butter, honey in
   1-quart Sauce Pan; heat over low heat
   until butter melts; blend; cool slightly;
   drizzle over popcorn mixture; toss
   together.

Makes 2 quarts

TOASTED POUND CAKE CUBES
A terrific "dip-it-yourself" dessert.

1 package (10¾-oz) frozen pound
  cake, thawed
¾ cup honey
1 tablespoon lemon juice
1 tablespoon butter or margarine
½ teaspoon lemon peel
2 tablespoons light rum
½ cup finely chopped walnuts

1. Cut cake into forty 1-inch cubes;
   allowing a 1-inch space from skewer
   handle, thread 5 cake cubes on each
   skewer; attach skewer guards.

2. Combine honey, lemon juice, butter,
   lemon peel in *1-quart Sauce Pan*; heat
   over medium heat until butter melts; stir
   in rum.

3. Insert skewers into *Kabob-It* base; place
   glass cover over food; kabob 5-6
   minutes or until cake is golden brown;
   dip cake cubes into sauce, then into
   chopped walnuts.

Makes 40

Variations:
May substitute chocolate 🍦 or fruit sauce 🍦,
and any chopped nuts or toasted coconut,
as desired.

MULLED WINE
Sit by a crackling fire with this warming
beverage.

2 cups sugar
2 cups water
3 cinnamon sticks
1 teaspoon whole cloves
3 medium oranges, thinly sliced
1 medium lemon, thinly sliced
½ cup raisins
¼ cup whole almonds
1 gallon Burgundy wine*

1. Combine sugar, water, cinnamon, cloves
   in *6-quart Electric Wok*; add orange and
   lemon slices, raisins, almonds; bring to
   boil on 300°F. setting; boil 5 minutes.

2. Reduce setting to 200°–225°F.; add
   wine; simmer until heated through,
   stirring occasionally. (Do not boil.)

Makes 5 quarts

*May substitute apple cider, as desired.

94

THE ITCH TO MAKE IT FROM SCRATCH

"I don't know what to do with all the tomatoes we got from our garden this year. We must have a barnful!"

"Why don't you make a big batch of sauce and freeze it? It tastes so much better than anything you can get at the store."

"Homemade is better" is an American axiom. Homemade baked goods, soups and stews are part of our basic heritage. Making meals "from scratch" hails from Colonial days when basic necessities were drawn from the environment by the resourcefulness and imagination of our ancestors.

Since contemporary life demands so much of people's time for work and interests outside the home, it is often much easier to use canned or frozen ingredients to complete a recipe. And yet when both time and inspiration are available in quantity, there is probably not a cook anywhere who doesn't like to roll up his or her sleeves and complete a recipe using fresh ingredients and some time-honored techniques.

The recipes in this chapter were created as a basis for many of the recipes you will find throughout this book. Most of our "scratch" recipes have a commercially packaged substitute that is widely available.

However, if you have a garden of fresh produce that needs a recipe, or you've got the time for simmering your own broth or preparing your own crepes, we hope this chapter satisfies your craving for a back-to-basics approach to food preparation. ■

95

BROTHS: According to Escoffier, food is only as good as the broth used in making it. If you don't start out with a good broth, no matter what the other ingredients are, your food will not be as tasty.

Broths can be concentrated at a 4 to 1 ratio (i.e., 1 quart to 1 cup) and kept frozen for later use. (If frozen, broth must be boiled immediately after defrosting.) They may be used in their concentrated forms for giving extra flavor when making sauces, or they may be reconstituted by simply adding water.

Broths can be used as building blocks for soups, stews, sauces and gravies.

CHICKEN BROTH

Simmers for hours; once it's in the pot, it's easy.

1	stewing chicken (3-lb)
5	quarts cold water
6	large carrots, halved
3	large onions, halved
4	green onions, halved
2	celery stalks, halved
1	tablespoon salt
1	teaspoon thyme
1	bay leaf
1	teaspoon parsley stems
6	peppercorns

1. Place chicken in *8½-quart Sauce Pot;* add water, carrots, onions, celery, salt, thyme, bay leaf, parsley; cover; bring to boil over medium-high heat; reduce heat to low; simmer 3-4 hours; add peppercorns last hour. (As liquid evaporates, replace with boiling water.)

2. Strain broth; cool slightly, then refrigerate overnight; lift off top layer of hardened fat; discard; store broth in air-tight containers in refrigerator or freezer.

Makes 4 quarts

BEEF BROTH

A great use for leftover beef bones.

3	pounds stewing beef or veal
3	pounds beef bones
4	quarts cold water
4	large carrots, halved
2	large onions, halved
2	green onions, halved
1	celery stalk, halved
1	bay leaf
1	tablespoon salt
1	teaspoon thyme
1	teaspoon parsley stems

1. Preheat *8½-quart Sauce Pot* over medium heat 2 minutes or until drops of water dance on hot pan surface; add meat; sauté until golden brown; add water; bring to boil; skim off top occasionally.

2. Add bones; simmer 30 minutes; skim; add vegetables, seasonings; simmer 6-8 hours. (As liquid evaporates, replace with boiling water.)

3. Strain broth; color with liquid browning sauce, as desired; cool slightly, then refrigerate overnight; lift off top layer of hardened fat; discard; store broth in air-tight containers in refrigerator or freezer.

Makes 4 quarts

QUICK BEEF BROTH

Better than canned, and very easy to make.

1½	pounds lean ground beef*
5	cups cold water
2	medium carrots, chopped
2	medium onions, chopped
1	bay leaf
1	teaspoon salt
½	teaspoon thyme
3	peppercorns

1. Combine beef, water in *3-quart Sauce Pan;* bring slowly to boil over medium heat; add vegetables, seasonings; skim off top occasionally; reduce heat to low; simmer 1 hour. (As liquid evaporates, replace with boiling water.)

2. Strain broth; color with liquid browning sauce, as desired; cool slightly, then refrigerate overnight; lift off top layer of hardened fat; discard; store broth in air-tight containers in refrigerator or freezer.

Makes 1 quart

*May substitute ground veal or giblets.

97

SAUCES: Basic sauces are building blocks or "mother sauces," but they can also be used as they stand. By varying the seasonings and adding different ingredients, you can create a variety of sauces from the basic recipes.

FRESH TOMATO SAUCE

Here's what to do with a bountiful crop from your own garden.

10	**pounds fresh ripe tomatoes**
¼	**cup vegetable oil**
2	**cups chopped onions**
1	**tablespoon salt**
2	**teaspoons pepper**

1. Cut tomatoes in half; roughly chop; heat oil in *5-quart Dutch Oven* over medium heat; sauté onions 5-6 minutes or until translucent; add tomatoes, salt, pepper; cover; cook 1 hour.

2. Remove cover; continue cooking 2½-3 hours, stirring occasionally, or until tomatoes are soft, sauce is thick; ladle mixture into blender container, in several batches; blend on low speed until smooth; strain as desired.

Makes 2 quarts

CANNED TOMATO SAUCE

An alternative to fresh when the grocer's aren't satisfactory.

¼	**cup vegetable oil**
2	**cups chopped onions**
3	**cans (2-lb, 3-oz each) tomatoes**
3¼	**quarts water**
2	**cans (6-oz each) tomato paste**
	Salt, pepper

1. Heat oil in *5-quart Dutch Oven* over medium heat; sauté onions 5-6 minutes or until translucent.

2. Add tomatoes, water, tomato paste; season with salt, pepper to taste; simmer 2½-3 hours or until slightly thick; strain as desired.

Makes 4 quarts

Tip:
Both these sauces can be frozen for 4-6 months.

These basic tomato sauces are sometimes referred to as "couli" or "fondue" and can be finished in a number of ways.

Variations:
• Traditional Italian—add garlic, basil, oregano and Parmesan cheese to taste. To be served with pasta.

• Provincial—add fennel seed, grated orange peel, garlic, basil and oregano to taste. Ideal with seafood.

• Marinara—add minced anchovy fillets or paste with traditional Italian seasonings for a spicy sauce for pasta or seafood.

• Shrimp—combination of equal parts of tomato and white sauces, with the addition of cooked shrimp and mushrooms, Worcestershire sauce, salt and pepper to taste.

• Tomato sauce may be enriched by adding butter or heavy cream.

HOLLANDAISE

Basic lemon, butter and egg sauce that's great with fish and vegetables.

⅓	cup water
1	tablespoon lemon juice
1	teaspoon salt
¼	teaspoon white pepper
3	egg yolks, well beaten
½	pound unsalted butter, melted
	Salt

1. Combine water, lemon juice, salt, pepper in *2-quart Sauce Pan;* cook over medium heat 10-12 minutes or until 2 tablespoons remain; add egg yolks; beat over low heat 2 minutes or until mixture becomes thick.

2. Remove from heat; add hot butter, drop by drop, beating with wooden spoon or plastic whisk until smooth, thickened; (add additional water, up to 2 tablespoons, if sauce becomes too thick); season with salt to taste; serve at once or keep warm in covered bowl.

Makes about 1½ cups

Tips:
• This sauce should be used immediately; however, if allowed to stand, keep warm and covered.
• On standing, butter may separate. This is easily corrected by adding a small amount of lukewarm water and whisking vigorously.

• If sauce curdles, blend 1 teaspoon cornstarch with 3 tablespoons water and add to the sauce. Bring to a boil, stirring constantly. This stabilizes the sauce, but will alter the true flavor of the sauce.

Variations:
• Mousseline Sauce—add ½ cup whipped heavy cream to 1 cup hollandaise.
• Mikado Sauce—substitute tangerine juice for lemon juice. Good served with seafood.
• Béarnaise Sauce—substitute vinegar for lemon juice and add tarragon and minced onions to taste.

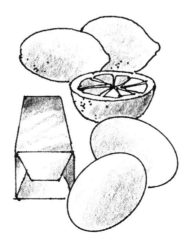

WHITE SAUCE

Béchamel, the basic building block for any cream sauce.

½	cup butter or margarine
½	cup flour
4½	cups milk, scalded
½	bay leaf
2	teaspoons salt
½	teaspoon white pepper
¼	teaspoon nutmeg
	Pinch thyme

1. Melt butter in *3-quart Sauce Pan* over medium heat; stir in flour with wooden spoon; cook 3 minutes, beating constantly.

2. Remove from heat; gradually add ½ the milk, beating until thoroughly combined; add remaining milk; beat until smooth; add seasonings.

3. Simmer 30 minutes over low heat, stirring occasionally; remove bay leaf; cool, then refrigerate or freeze unused portion; if frozen, reheat gradually.

Makes 1 quart

Variations:
• Thin White—use 2 tablespoons each butter and flour to 1 cup milk.
• Thick White—use ¼ cup each butter and flour to 1 cup milk.
• Mornay—add ¼ cup shredded hard or semi-soft cheese (Gruyère, Cheddar, Parmesan).
• Pasta—add crumbled Bleu, Roquefort or Gorgonzola cheese to taste and serve over pasta.

99

BATTERS: Batters are easy to make, but a bit of technique will insure perfection. Crepe batter is almost the opposite of pancake batter. Because crepes are thin it is important that the gluten be developed to hold them together; therefore, the batter should be beaten for about 5 minutes. On the other hand, pancakes should be light and fluffy; the batter should just be mixed together until moistened. Other types of flours can be used to make crepes and pancakes. To save time, dry ingredients can be put together and stored in plastic bags, then used when needed by simply adding liquid ingredients.

PANCAKES

A homemade variety that's as easy as the packaged mixes.

1¼	**cups all purpose flour**
2	**tablespoons sugar**
2	**teaspoons baking powder**
½	**teaspoon grated lemon peel**
¼	**teaspoon salt**
1	**egg, slightly beaten**
1¼	**cups light cream or milk**
3	**tablespoons butter or margarine, melted**

1. In medium bowl, combine flour, sugar, baking powder, lemon peel, salt; add egg, cream, butter; mix until just blended —will be slightly lumpy.

2. Place *Double Griddle* over two units of range; preheat over medium heat about 2 minutes or until drops of water dance on dry griddle surface.

3. Pour by ¼ cupful onto ungreased griddle (6 at a time); turn after 2 minutes or when bubbles break on top; continue cooking 1 minute or until cakes are golden brown—adjust heat as needed.

Makes 12

CREPES

Every culture has its own version of crepe; these will freeze well.

¾	**cup all purpose flour**
3	**eggs**
1	**cup milk**
¼	**cup butter or margarine, melted**
½	**teaspoon salt**

1. With electric mixer at low speed, beat flour, eggs 4-6 minutes or until mixture is shiny; gradually add milk, continuing to beat until blended; stir in butter, salt; let stand 20 minutes.

2. Preheat *8-inch Chef Style Fry Pan* over medium heat 2 minutes or until drops of water dance on dry pan surface; for each crepe, pour about 2 tablespoons batter into pan; immediately tilt pan to coat bottom evenly; cook 45 seconds or until top looks dry; turn; cook second side about 20 seconds.

3. Fill crepes with any savory or sweet filling, as desired; may be served as an entree or dessert.

Makes 12

Tip:
• Crepes may be made ahead for later use —cool on wire racks; stack between sheets of waxed paper; wrap securely in freezer paper or plastic wrap; freeze up to 3 months; thaw overnight in refrigerator.

Variations:
• Buckwheat—substitute buckwheat flour for ½ the regular flour.
• Whole Wheat—substitute ⅓ whole wheat flour for the regular flour.
• Oatmeal—soften ½ cup quick-cooking oats in a little milk; reduce regular flour by 2 tablespoons.
• Any combination of fruits, nuts, seasonings may be added to pancake batter, as desired.

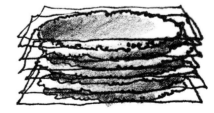

100

STIRRED CUSTARD

You don't need a double-boiler to make the old-fashioned treat.

¼	cup sugar
4	egg yolks
	Pinch salt
1	cup milk, scalded
1	teaspoon vanilla

1. Gradually beat sugar into egg yolks using whisk; continue to beat 1 minute longer once all sugar has been added; pour mixture into *2-quart Sauce Pan;* gradually add slightly cooled scalded milk, salt; cook over medium-low heat, stirring constantly with wooden spoon (using figure 8 motion) until almost all the tiny bubbles have disappeared from surface of custard, about 9-10 minutes.

2. Remove from heat, but continue to stir for 1 minute longer (mixture should have thickened, will coat the spoon); add vanilla; pour into serving dishes; serve warm or cool slightly, then refrigerate.

Makes 1½ cups

Tips:
• The figure 8 motion is very important as it moves all the liquid evenly in the pan.
• When making larger quantities, eggs will continue to cook unless removed from the pan immediately and whisked.
• To make the famous Crème Brûlée, substitute heavy cream for milk and top with brown sugar; place under preheated broiler for 1-2 minutes.

Variation:
May substitute 1 teaspoon of your favorite liqueur for vanilla.

PRALINE POWDER

An easy way to add nutty flavor to any dessert.

2	cups sugar
¾	cup water
¼	teaspoon lemon juice
2	cups chopped hazelnuts*

1. Combine sugar, water, lemon juice in *2-quart Sauce Pan;* cook over medium heat; after 10 minutes of cooking, watch carefully; when mixture begins to turn brown, remove from heat immediately.

2. Add nuts; pour mixture onto *15½ x 12-inch Cookie Sheet;* with 2 forks, lift and pull mixture into 14 x 12-inch rectangle; cool; break into pieces; place in food processor or blender in several batches; pulverize to a sand-like texture; store in air-tight container.

Makes 3 cups

*To remove skins, spread nuts evenly in shallow bake pan; bake 20 minutes at 400°F.; pour onto cloth towel; rub to remove skins.

Tips:
• Essentially this is a flavored sugar that can be used in or on anything as a replacement for sugar, giving an extra-rich flavor to the product.
• Any variety of nut may be used, although hazelnuts are traditional in European cooking and have the richest flavor.

MERINGUE SHELLS

Sweet, crunchy individual serving shells made from egg whites.

3	egg whites (room temperature)
¼	teaspoon cream of tartar
¾	cup sugar
½	teaspoon vanilla

1. With electric mixer at high speed, beat egg whites, cream of tartar until foamy; add sugar (2 tablespoons at a time), continuing to beat until stiff, glossy peaks form (about 10-15 minutes); blend in vanilla.

2. Using ½ meringue mixture, make 4 mounds on *15½ x 12-inch Cookie Sheet;* spread each mound into a 3-inch circle, ¼-inch thick.

3. Fill barrel of *Super Shooter* with remaining meringue mixture; make ¾-inch sides around meringue circles in fluted design using decorator tip.

4. Bake 60-75 minutes at 250°F. or until shells are crisp, dry; turn oven off; leave in oven 1 hour longer to dry thoroughly; cool completely on cookie sheet.

Makes 4

Tips:
• You cannot beat egg whites successfully unless all equipment is clean and grease-free, and there is no yolk in the whites.
• To maintain shape and volume of meringue shells, place immediately into preheated oven.
• For chocolate meringue shells, add a small amount of unsweetened cocoa powder to meringue mixture.

BREAD: Like many aspects of cooking, the key to successful breadmaking is experience. There are several factors which can cause your results to vary: temperature, humidity and altitude are some examples. And only experience will tell you exactly when a dough is wet enough or when it has been kneaded sufficiently.

When making bread dough, remember these points:
- Yeast is a living organism that is subject to temperature. Too cold a temperature will make yeast lazy or put it to sleep, while too high a temperature will kill it.
- Humidity will affect the amount of flour a dough will need. On a rainy or very humid day, you may need to add extra flour, but never more than ½ cup. On a day when the air is dry, you may need to cut the amount of flour used.
- Kneading is a technique that, with practice, will become second nature. A dough has been kneaded sufficiently when it is smooth and slightly tacky to the touch. Under-kneading will result in a heavy, soggy bread; over-kneading usually results in a coarse, uneven texture.
- Allow bread to rise in a section of the kitchen that is free from drafts for even rising. Place dough in a lightly greased large ceramic or glass bowl. Cover the rising dough to prevent it from drying out.
- Dough must double in bulk before shaping. To check, poke two fingers an inch into the dough. If depressions remain, dough is ready to shape.

BASIC WHITE BREAD
Once you've mastered it, you'll never go back to the bakery!

3	**cups all purpose flour**
2	**tablespoons sugar**
4	**teaspoons salt**
2	**packages active dry yeast**
2	**cups water**
¼	**cup vegetable oil**
3½	**cups all purpose flour**

1. In large bowl, thoroughly mix flour, sugar, salt, yeast.

2. Heat water, oil in *1-quart Sauce Pan* until very warm (120°-130°F.); gradually add to dry ingredients using low speed of electric mixer; beat 2 minutes on medium speed; add 2 cups flour; beat 2 minutes on high speed, scraping bowl occasionally; with spoon, stir in additional flour to make stiff dough.

3. Turn dough out onto lightly floured board; knead 8-10 minutes or until smooth, elastic; place in greased bowl; cover with towel; let rise 45 minutes or until doubled in bulk.

4. Punch down dough until all air is forced out; divide in half; shape into 2 loaves; place in two *8½ x 4 x 3-inch Loaf Pans;* cover with towel; let rest until doubled in bulk.

5. Bake 40 minutes at 375°F. or until golden brown, bread sounds hollow when tapped with finger.

Makes 2 loaves

Variations:

French-Style Loaf
Divide dough in half; roll each piece into 13 x 12-inch rectangle; roll rectangles tightly to form long loaves; taper ends by rolling them back and forth in palm of hands; place diagonally on *15½ x 12-inch Cookie Sheets;* make diagonal slashes on top of loaves; cover with towel; let rest 30 minutes. Bake 20-25 minutes at 425°F. or until golden brown, bread sounds hollow when tapped with finger.

Pizza Bread
Divide dough in half; place pieces on two *15½ x 12-inch Cookie Sheets;* roll into 13 x 12-inch rectangles; cover with towel; let rest 30 minutes; make indentations across top of bread with thumb; fill with olive oil; sprinkle with coarse salt, sage, finely minced garlic (optional); bake 25-30 minutes at 425°F. or until golden brown.

FLAVORED BUTTERS

The simplest of "sauces" for any dish.

½ cup butter

1. With electric mixer, beat butter until light, fluffy; blend in appropriate seasonings (see following recipes).
2. Fill barrel of *Super Shooter* with butter mixture; pipe rosettes 1 x ¾-inch onto waxed paper using decorator tip; refrigerate or freeze until serving time.

Makes about 1½ dozen

Caraway Mustard Butter
Great with pork and lamb.

1 tablespoon Dijon mustard
2 teaspoons chopped caraway seeds
Salt, pepper

Cajun Butter
Goes well with both seafood and beef.

2 tablespoons minced green onions
2 teaspoons lime juice
1 teaspoon Tabasco sauce
Salt, pepper

Mint Butter
Just perfect with lamb, or green peas.

1 tablespoon chopped fresh mint
2 teaspoons lemon juice
Salt, pepper

Dill Butter
A mate for salmon and other fish; good with vegetables, too.

1 tablespoon chopped fresh dill
2 teaspoons lemon juice
Salt, pepper

FRUIT SAUCE

A fine addition to most desserts; will keep in the refrigerator.

3 large nectarines, peeled, sliced
3 large plums, peeled, sliced
1 cup fresh orange juice
½ cup sugar (optional)
¼ cup brandy (optional)

1. Combine nectarines, plums, orange juice in *2-quart Sauce Pan;* bring to boil over medium heat; simmer over low heat 30 minutes or until fruit is soft, most of liquid is gone.
2. Remove from heat; stir in sugar, brandy.
3. Serve hot or cold over ice cream, pound cake, plain pastries, fresh berries, cut-up fruit, pancakes, crepes, waffles, custards, puddings or omelets.

Makes 2 cups

Tips:
• An excellent way to use overripe fruits.
• Any fresh fruit may be substituted for the nectarines, and any dried fruit for plums.
• Any other spirit or liqueur may be substituted for brandy, and any other fruit juice for orange juice.

GARNISHING — THE PROFESSIONAL TOUCH

The ultimate success of any recipe goes beyond just the taste of the food; the dish should have eye appeal as well. Decorative embellishments that enhance foods and make them more appetizing are called garnishes. A garnish may be as simple as a sprig of fresh herb, as succulent as thin slices of mushroom sautéed in butter, or as intricate as perfectly-veined leaves of bitter chocolate. Here are some ideas for garnishes and instructions on how to make them:

- **Sprigs of fresh herbs** such as anise, chive, dill, fennel, coriander (often referred to as Chinese parsley), lavender, oregano, marjoram, parsley, rosemary, sorrel, sage and thyme. Any of these herbs, used whole as sprigs or chopped, can dress up the look of a plate and add a fresh, unmistakable flavor as well. Use your favorites to decorate meat, fish and poultry dishes, as well as soups and stews.

- **Leaves or tops of vegetables** such as carrot, celery or radish. Normally discarded, these garnishes add color and texture to foods.

- **Leaves of greens** such as lettuce, spinach or watercress. Used as beds for cold salads, these greens form a perfect frame for any culinary picture.

- **Chiffonade of leafy vegetables** such as lettuce or spinach. These long curly strips make a bed for presenting cold foods, such as Marinated Swordfish, Marinated Mushrooms or Chicken Liver Mousse.

    To cut a chiffonade, roll several leaves together, and slice the rolls at $1/8$-inch intervals.

- **Grated zest of citrus fruits** such as lime, orange and lemon. (The zest is the colorful outer peel.) In addition to its decorative color, grated zest also adds a tangy flavor of its own.

- **Julienne of vegetables** such as carrot, zucchini or summer squash. Now the darling of nouvelle cuisine, these thin strips can be cooked quickly to retain full flavor, color and healthiness.

    To cut vegetables into a julienne, first cut into $1/8$-inch slices. Then cut lengthwise across each slice into sticks, $1/16$ to $1/8$-inch wide. Cut strips into 2-inch lengths.

- **Mirepoix or brunoise of vegetables** such as peppers. These small squares of vegetables are used both raw and cooked to add texture and color to dishes.

    To cut into mirepoix, first cut vegetables into julienne, then cut across julienne into small cubes, $1/16$ to $1/8$-inch square.

- **Scallion brushes.** Use to garnish Oriental dishes, or wherever a graceful garnish is desired.

    To make, remove root end of scallion or green onion. Cut off a piece 3 inches in length and make shallow slashes into the sides of scallion piece, about 2 inches in length. Place scallion brush in cold water for 3-5 minutes to allow it to curl.

- **Chocolate leaves.** Select a leaf with prominent veins such as a fresh mint leaf. Melt several squares of chocolate, depending on number of leaves needed. Using a small metal spatula or knife, spread chocolate on underside of leaf to about $1/8$-inch thickness, being careful not to allow any chocolate to drip onto the front side of the leaf. Lay chocolate side up on waxed paper and refrigerate until chocolate is well hardened, about 10-15 minutes. Working quickly, carefully peel leaf away from hardened chocolate, then return chocolate leaf to refrigerator 1-2 minutes longer. Use to garnish any dessert.

EASY DOES IT— SOME HELPFUL COOKING HINTS

Listing Ingredients
• In all recipes the ingredients are listed in order of use.

Proper Tools
• When cooking in SilverStone coated pans, wooden or plastic kitchen tools (spoons, spatulas, knives and whisks) are recommended to protect the non-stick surface.

Seasonings
• All recipes were developed with minimal seasoning and may need adjusting for personal taste. Correct seasoning at the end of cooking. Cold foods will often require additional seasonings.

• When herbs are dried, their flavor intensifies. Use half as much of the dried herbs as of the fresh. It is advisable to date your herbs and spices when you buy them. Optimum flavor will remain up to 6 months.

• Don't throw away those parsley stems as they provide lots of flavor for soups, stews and broths. They may be kept in the refrigerator or frozen for later use.

• Overseasoning can be corrected. If you find that a dish is too salty, add an acid such as lemon juice or vinegar. If too acidic, add salt.

Room Temperature Ingredients
• Especially in baking, all ingredients should be at room temperature for best results. For example, egg whites will give greater volume when beaten at room temperature.

Measuring Unsifted Flour
• Lightly spoon flour into measuring cup. (Do not pack.) Level off with a straight metal spatula.

Butter
• Clarified—Commonly served with seafood, artichokes and asparagus and excellent for sautéeing to prevent overbrowning.
  To prepare, melt butter over low heat. Remove from heat and let settle. Skim off and discard butterfat on top; spoon out butter, being careful not to disturb any of the sediment (milk solids) at the bottom.

• As a thickener—Because of certain properties found in butter, it is an excellent thickener for sauces. Margarine contains more oil and therefore will not perform as well. However, where indicated, you may substitute margarine for butter in many of these recipes.

• Salted vs. unsalted—Salt in butter acts as a preservative, thereby extending shelf life. Foods will brown more easily in salted butter. The choice is a matter of individual taste. Both salted and unsalted butter can be frozen.

Fresh / Frozen Vegetables
• In most cases, frozen vegetables may be substituted for fresh. If using frozen vegetables, add near the end of cooking whenever possible to avoid overcooked, mushy textures.

Oils
• Use olive oil when preparing Italian or Mediterranean dishes. The subtle yet distinctive flavor of olive oil gives an authentic touch.

• Use vegetable oil when deep fat frying. The high smoking point and bland flavor will not interfere with the food being fried. You can strain the oil used in frying and reuse, providing the same foods will be fried. For example, oil used for frying fish will not be suitable for frying potatoes.

Milk / Cream / Yogurt
• In some cases, you may want to experiment by interchanging milk, cream, sour cream and yogurt in salad dressing, sauces and soups. However, a few words of caution. When adding sour cream or yogurt to a hot dish, add at the end of the cooking, just heating through. Do not boil. Also, mix yogurt lightly into a sauce or dressing. Overmixing will cause the yogurt to break down.

Stir-Frying
• Method of cooking small, evenly cut pieces of meats and vegetables in a small amount of oil over high heat. It is important to toss foods continuously for tender-crisp vegetables and juicy, tender meats.

Check For Doneness
• Poultry—The juices should run clear when sharp knife is inserted behind leg.
• Fish—Flesh should flake when lightly touched with a fork.
• Shellfish—Clams, mussels, etc. are done when shells open wide. (Do not eat any that have not opened wide.)
• Shrimp—Shrimp are done when they curl up and become pink. (Overcooking will toughen.)
• Lobster—As a general rule, an average size lobster (1-2 lb) is done when boiled 12-15 minutes. The shell should be bright red.
• Meats—Meats should be nicely browned on one side, then turned and sprinkled with salt. When blood comes to the top and meat feels slightly firm to the touch, it's rare. As meat continues to cook it will become firmer.
• Pasta—Pasta should be "al dente" or with slight firmness, not mushy. It is best cooked in a large quantity of salted water for even cooking. A tablespoon of oil may be added to the water to prevent sticking. For best results, follow package directions.

Make Ahead
• Most soups, stews and casseroles taste best when prepared a day in advance. This will allow the flavors to develop.

Freezing
• Many of the recipes in this book may be made in advance and frozen. Wrap tightly, label and date each item. Thaw in microwave or in the refrigerator overnight.

Microwave Reheating
• Reheating in the microwave is best for dishes with high water content such as stews, soups and casseroles. It may be necessary to rotate the dish or give the food an occasional stir to distribute the heat evenly. Also, cover loosely with plastic wrap to retain moisture. Add additional liquid and adjust seasoning as desired before serving. Note: Bread and bread products may not reheat well in the microwave. It is best to consult the manufacturer's instructions for proper reheating.

109

APPROXIMATE EQUIVALENTS	
Pinch	Amount that can be held between thumb and forefinger
Dash	Less than $1/8$ teaspoon
1 pound unsifted all purpose flour	4 cups
1 ounce baking chocolate	1 square
1/4 pound nuts	1 cup chopped
1 cup raw rice	3 cups cooked
1 slice bread	1/2 cup bread crumbs
1 large onion	1 cup chopped
1 large green pepper	1/2 cup chopped
1 pound tomatoes	2 cups chopped
1 pound potatoes	2 1/4 cups diced or sliced
1/4 pound mushrooms	2 cups sliced
1 pound apples	3 cups sliced
1 pound bananas	1 1/3 cups mashed
1 medium lemon	3 tablespoons juice
1 medium orange	1/3-1/2 cup juice
1/4 pound cheese	1 cup shredded
1 cup heavy cream	2 cups whipped

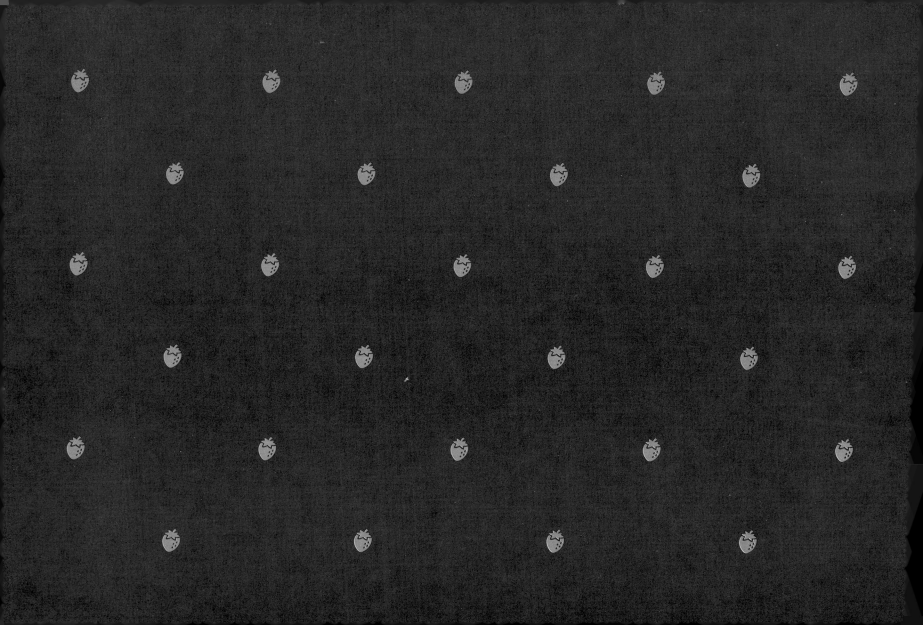

PUTTING IT ALL TOGETHER

FEAST MENUS

Every so often, you'll have occasion to prepare a feast. Whether it's a pre-wedding supper or a family reunion, a feast is a special meal, and we've developed some menu ideas to assist your planning.

Many of the feast recipes are contained in this cookbook; those that are not are easy to find in any basic cookbook, or you may already know how to make them.

Wine and other beverage suggestions are simply that—suggestions. Generally, "red wine with red meat, white wine with white meat or fish" is an easy rule to follow, but don't be afraid to break the rule if you like to experiment with wine.

Note:
Feast recipes from this cookbook are shown in capital letters.

ITALIAN FEAST

PIZZA BIANCA ~ antipasto
SCAMPI
braciole
spaghetti ~ ZUCCHINI BASILICO
Italian Soave
AMARETTO SOUFFLE
cappucino

NEW ENGLAND FEAST

OYSTER STEW
BOSTON-STYLE FISH CAKES
boiled lobster with clarified butter
cole slaw ~ French fries
beer or dry white wine
VERMONT BREAD PUDDING

COUNTRY FRENCH FEAST

FRENCH ONION SOUP
RILLETTE
GARDEN TERRINE
COQ AU VIN
parsley potatoes
tossed green salad
with vinaigrette dressing
red Burgundy
HONEY CUSTARD

ENGLISH FEAST

SHIRRED EGGS WITH CHEESE
TOAD-IN-THE-HOLE
fish and chips
steak and kidney pie
oven roasted potatoes
Brussels sprouts
red Bordeaux or hard cider
BERRY TRIFLE ~ BRANDY SNAPS

FEAST MENUS

ORIENTAL FEAST (Chinese)

hot and sour soup
ORIENTAL PORK TOASTS ~ fried wonton
CRISPY MUSHROOM DUCK
SZECHUAN CHICKEN
fried shrimp with oyster sauce
steamed rice
green beans Szechuan-style
Chinese beer or California Chablis
lichee nuts ~ fortune cookies
tea

NOUVELLE FRENCH FEAST

COLD WATERCRESS SOUP
POACHED SALMON
with
STIR-FRIED CUCUMBERS
lemon sorbet
CHICKEN IN CHAMPAGNE
VEGETABLES JARDINIERE
Champagne or California Chardonnay
kiwi tart

SPANISH FEAST

empanadas
SEAFOOD PAELLA
braised rabbit
sautéed mushrooms in garlic sauce
roasted potatoes
sherry, dry Spanish white or rosé wine
flan
espresso

LATIN FEAST

BLACK BEAN SOUP ~ white rice
fried red snapper
roast suckling pig
fried bananas
avocado and onion salad
beer or dry white wine
rice pudding

GREEK FEAST

LEMON SOUP
COLD MARINATED SWORDFISH
MOUSSAKA
rice pilaf
spinach salad with feta cheese and olives
Italian Chianti or Ouzo
baklava

TEX-MEX FEAST

BEAN DIP ~ guacamole
tortilla chips
MEXICAN MEATBALLS
chicken and sour cream enchiladas
refried beans ~ jalapeño peppers
Margaritas or Mexican beer
assorted sherbets

FEAST MENUS

SOUTHERN FEAST

seafood gumbo
SOUTHERN-STYLE CORNBREAD
southern fried chicken with cream gravy
barbequed pork ribs
black eyed peas~collard greens
Mint Juleps or rosé wine
sweet potato pie

ITALIAN FEAST II (northern)

SAVORY STUFFED ARTICHOKES
polenta with cheese (baked)
cold seafood salad
CHICKEN PICCATA
fried zucchini~braised fennel
dry white wine
cheeses
LEMON COOKIES
espresso

EAST INDIAN FEAST

lentil soup
deep fried potato dumplings
VEGETABLE CURRY
rice
yogurt, chutney,
mandarin oranges, coconut
poori (deep fried Indian bread)
California Chenin Blanc
fresh yogurt cheese in honey syrup
tea

WEAR-EVER:
THE BEST
FOR YOUR
KITCHEN

When it comes to cookware, nobody has more experience than Wear-Ever. For over 80 years, Wear-Ever has brought quality cookware and bakeware to the kitchens of America. And Wear-Ever brings that same quality to our line of specialty electric appliances.

With the kitchen becoming the focal point of the home in the 80s, and with a growing trend toward home entertaining and a greater emphasis on the family, quality cooking utensils and appliances are a must.

Relying on extra-heavy-gauge Wear-Ever Cookware and Bakeware with SilverStone has become second nature to those who take pride in the foods they turn out in their kitchens. The thick aluminum utensils cut down on cooking time and the non-stick SilverStone surface practically eliminates clean-up time, freeing today's busy people from kitchen chores and providing more time for leisure activities.

Having friends over for dinner is easier and more fun than it has ever been, and part of the fun is letting guests actually join in making their meal. Wear-Ever's line of specialty electrics lets them do just that— from "shooting" their own canapés with the Super Shooter to kabobbing their appetizers, entrées or desserts on the Kabob-It.

You've relied on Wear-Ever for 80 years because we've proven that the older we get, the better we cook. And you know you can continue relying on us.

Wear-Ever's the way to cook today!

Wear-Ever Cookware with SilverStone

No matter what you are in the mood to cook, chances are it will turn out better when you use Wear-Ever Cookware with SilverStone. Light weight, durable aluminum has been the material preferred by professional chefs for years because of its superior heat-conducting qualities. The thick, heavy-gauge aluminum spreads heat rapidly and evenly for consistent cooking results.

SilverStone, the incredibly tough non-stick cooking surface, is triple-bonded to Wear-Ever cookware at 800°F. This super slick surface requires little or no oil (great news for the diet-conscious). Compared to earlier DuPont non-stick

coatings, SilverStone is 30 to 50 percent thicker and offers improved resistance to scratching, peeling and chipping.

Our cookware is equipped with firm-fitting, heat-resistant phenolic handles, safe in the oven up to 350°F. And certain utensils with metal handles, such as the Au Gratin Pan or the Gourmet Style Fry Pan, are perfect for top broiling to melt cheese or to brown crumb toppings.

The recipes in this book were developed specifically for Wear-Ever Cookware with SilverStone. For best results, always use these utensils.

Wear-Ever Bakeware with SilverStone

Stocking your kitchen with quality bakeware from Wear-Ever is the first step in turning out quality baked goods.

Our heavy-gauge aluminum bakeware offers uniform heating, especially important for baked goods. When baked in an aluminum pan, cakes, coffee cakes, quick breads and yeast breads brown evenly on the sides and bottom for uniform results with good volume.

The SilverStone surface on Wear-Ever Bakeware allows breads, cakes, rolls and biscuits to turn right out of the pan—a major advancement in baking. Although recipes with a high sugar content, such as some cakes and quick breads, still require greasing and flouring the pan, clean-up is a breeze!

Since exact measurements are crucial in bakeware (pan size alone can determine the success or failure of many recipes), dimensions are stamped on the bottom of Wear-Ever Premium Bakeware.

The recipes in this book were developed specifically for Wear-Ever Bakeware with SilverStone. For best results, always use these bakeware items.

Wear-Ever Popcorn Pumper

The Wear-Ever Popcorn Pumper, the first electric hot air home cornpopper, is America's best! In comparative evaluations of five national brands of hot air cornpoppers by an independent testing laboratory, our Popcorn Pumper was rated No. 1. It pops both standard and gourmet brands of corn in hot air, not hot oil. The Popcorn Pumper pops bigger, fluffier batches in three short minutes with no oily mess. And because it's portable and so easy to operate, you can use the Pumper in almost any room in the house.

The large popping chamber allows the corn to receive a maximum amount of heat and air for a shorter popping time, but the kernels stay in motion so they don't burn.

The cornhopper in the top of the chute automatically measures one-half cup of popcorn which yields a 3½ to 5 quart batch depending on the variety of corn used. The transparent yellow thermoplastic chute allows for an even flow of popped corn into the bowl, and needs only occasional cleaning in sudsy water.

Popcorn is a healthy snack. It has high fiber content, and when eaten without butter, it has few calories. However, for butter lovers, the large butter cup can melt three tablespoons of butter at a time. The butter cup handle is black thermoplastic and remains cool.

Based on the national average cost of electricity, using the Popcorn Pumper to pop two batches of corn a week for a full year will cost only 33¢.

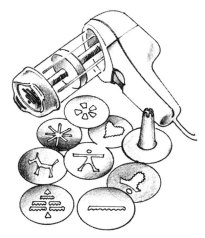

Wear-Ever Super Shooter

The Wear-Ever Super Shooter is an electric cookie, canapé and candy maker. This unique, energy-efficient electric foodgun comes with a decorator tip, filler tip, nine cookie discs and two barrels.

The Super Shooter is easy to load, easy to use and easy to clean.

Load the barrel with cookie dough, cheeses and spreads, or fillings for pasta, tomatoes, deviled eggs or pastry for beautiful and imaginative results. It shoots appetizers, entrées, garnishes, desserts and candy.

Using this portable, energy-efficient foodgun once a week for one year will cost less than a penny.

The Super Shooter gives picture-perfect results that look hard to achieve but aren't. It triggers a whole new era of ease and convenience in the kitchen.

Wear-Ever Kabob-It

The Wear-Ever Kabob-It, an electric hot hors d'oeuvre/meal maker, was designed for the casual eating styles of the 80s. Fun to watch, easy to clean and portable, Kabob-It is perfect for entertaining friends, serving exotic or everyday meals, or feeding an active family in shifts.

Eight vertical skewers rotate on their own axes slowly around a central heating element to kabob meat, fish, vegetables and fruits. The self-cleaning heating element broils foods at 400°F. The vertical design allows juices and marinades to drip slowly from the foods for lower-calorie, spatter-free results.

The PYREX® brand glass cover protects the food and contains the heat for even cooking. The removable drip tray features a SilverStone surface that makes clean-up easy by allowing excess juices to drain into an easy-cleaning, removable drip cup.

Using the Kabob-It once a week for an entire year will cost just 65¢.

With the Kabob-It, entertaining takes a turn for the better and skewer cooking becomes an exciting visual experience.

®PYREX is the registered trademark of Corning Glass Works

Wear-Ever Electric Wok

The secret of the Wear-Ever Electric Wok is its unique shape, curved sides with a small flat area in the bottom, and its material, aluminum. Rapid, even heating turns out seafood, poultry, meats and tender-but-crunchy vegetables to Oriental perfection. High heat is concentrated in the flat bottom area.

The six-quart Electric Wok has a SilverStone surface and a heat control probe for accurate and predictable performance. The unit is completely immersible for easy cleaning when the heat control is detached.

The sparkling porcelain-coated base and cover, finished in Oriental red or almond, are durable and fade resistant. Using the Electric Wok once a week for a full year costs only 39¢.

This versatile appliance can be used for searing, simmering, sautéing, stir-frying, deep-frying, braising, poaching and steaming. It can also be used as a hot pot for classic fondue, as a punch bowl or even as a salad bowl. It's the best friend a creative cook ever had!

Wear-Ever Low Pressure Cooker/Pressure Fryer

Quick and easy pressure cooking with this 6-quart Low Pressure Cooker/Pressure Fryer is the way to bring out all the nutritious flavor of meats and vegetables. This appliance is the only pressure cooker that is so safe, it's a pressure fryer, too!

The Cooker cooks foods at 5 to 6 pounds of pressure and has a regulator on the cover that maintains the correct pressure. Four safety vents around the edge of the cover allow any excess pressure to escape if the regulator's vent tube becomes clogged. The sturdy clamp and bracket cover device provides a tight, secure fit.

The Cooker reduces normal cooking time by a third for more efficient range-top cooking. It can also be used for deep fat frying without mess or spatter.

Whether pressure cooking family favorites or more exotic fare, the Pressure Cooker/Pressure Fryer is just what you need for last-minute entertaining or preparing family meals in a hurry.

118

NDEX

119

128

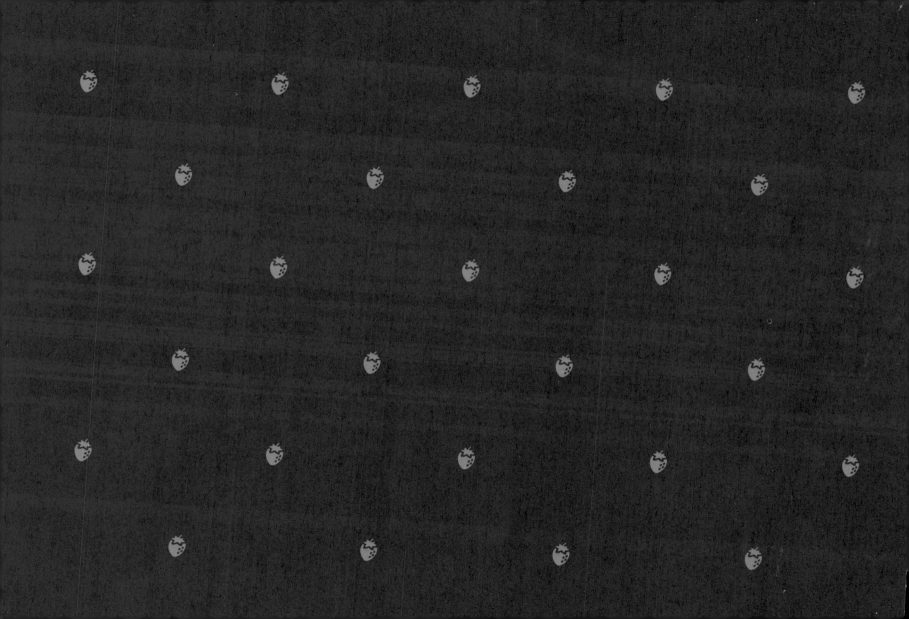